The KITCHEN
GARDEN

The KITCHEN GARDEN

Fresh Ideas for Luscious Vegetables, Herbs, Flowers, and Fruit

NORMA CONEY

FRIEDMAN/FAIRFAX
PUBLISHERS

A FRIEDMAN/FAIRFAX BOOK

Friedman/Fairfax Publishers
15 West 26 Street
New York, NY 10010
Telephone (212) 685-6610
Fax (212) 685-1307
Please visit our website: www.metrobooks.com

Library of Congress Cataloging-in-Publication Data available upon request.

ISBN 1-58663-012-1

Editor: Susan Lauzau
Art Director: Jeff Batzli
Designer: Amanda Wilson
Photography Editor: Wendy Missan
Production Director: Karen Matsu Greenberg

Color separations by Radstock Repro
Printed in Hong Kong by Midas Printing Co. Ltd.

1 3 5 7 9 10 8 6 4 2

Distributed by Sterling Publishing Co., Inc.
387 Park Avenue South
New York, NY 10016-8810
Orders and customer service (800) 367-9692
Fax: (800) 542-7567
E-mail: custservice@sterlingpub.com
Website: www.sterlingpublishing.com

contents

introduction

The kitchen garden as a design theme is today enjoying a spirited renaissance. After a period of contempt for the useful and an elevation of the ornamental, gardeners are returning to the age-old tradition of mixed plantings of vegetables, herbs, and flowers.

The most important function of a kitchen garden is to produce fresh food for the gardener's table. Thus, a kitchen garden is likely to include vegetables, fruits large and small, herbs for flavor and health, and even fresh flowers, which add color to both the table and the garden. A given garden may include all of these types of plants, or it may feature plants from just one or two of these categories.

The design of a kitchen garden will be as individual as the gardener who plants it. There are historical precedents and, of course, common sense dictates certain guidelines, but other than that there are no set rules regarding layout. Trends toward or away from formality, waxing and waning influences of various cultures, and the

Victorian gardens, like this walled kitchen garden, were lushly designed and filled with many types of vegetables, herbs, and flowers.

rediscovery of gardening methods and designs from different time periods all contribute to a range of kitchen garden styles that are coming in or going out of fashion at any given time. But whatever the chosen style, the simple fact that each backyard is different in size, shape, and soil type helps each kitchen garden attain a look all its its own.

Kitchen gardens are one of the oldest types of gardens, but exactly how far back in time they date is hard to judge. There is little doubt that as humans became less nomadic and began to live in one dwelling for long periods of time, tending a patch of vegetables became a reliable means of supplementing a diet that was otherwise subject to the whims of nature. Over the millennia, people gained a fair amount of horticultural wisdom, and came to understand what should be planted when, where, and with what other plants in order to ensure the largest and healthiest crop. Gardeners in subsequent generations have been the beneficiaries of this knowledge.

Several periods of history have produced noteworthy gardens in the extreme. Cloistered monasteries during the Dark Ages had such gardens. These monasteries became beacons of light and enlightenment in an age when Europe was languishing physically and intellectually, and suffering the attacks of barbaric peoples. Monks tended these gardens to provide "meate fore the table" for themselves and for peasants who sought refuge from barbarians within their walls. Included in these monastery gardens were herb gardens, referred to as physic gardens. In fact, monasteries were responsible for keeping a working knowledge of the medicinal tendencies of herbs alive during this dark period in European history. By the Middle Ages, this horticultural expertise had been passed on to a new generation of herbalists.

In colonial America, another example of kitchen gardens emerged. Thrust into an unfamiliar land, those bound for America knew not what they would find. Every effort was made to bring both seed and plant material from the old country to provide for the necessities of life. Everything from vegetables and tonic herbs to dye plants, medicinal plants, and fiber plants such as flax were sown in the dooryard. Even a few poisonous plants flourished in these gardens driven by self-sufficiency. As years went by, these colonial gardens came to include native species, recommended by the native American Indians for both medicinal purposes and food production.

By far the most extravagant examples of what kitchen gardens can encompass was achieved in Victorian England. Near the close of the nineteenth century, kitchen gardens and some of the horticultural techniques that made them hum, were at their peak. A garden on a Victorian estate went far beyond the realm of what is practical today, and was made possible by unimaginable wealth.

Such a garden might have included a vegetable plot for fresh garden produce, a fruit garden for in-season fruits, a vineyard and winery, a mushroom house, greenhouses for growing seedlings, a series of elaborate cold frames, beds for herbs and flowers perhaps formally arranged, a rose garden, and perhaps a conservatory for producing a fresh supply of potted plants for the house. Some or most of these gardens would be walled off with brick or high hedges to protect the garden from bad weather early and late in the year. Special greenhouses were erected for the production of melons and exotic fruits such as peaches and apricots. Citrus fruits were grown under glass year round. The head gardener may have been called upon to produce a favorite flower for the lady of the house all year long. Fresh flower bouquets were picked for the house from the cutting garden. The demands were many on the head gardener, who oversaw a staff of his own.

Produce was stored for use out of season, sometimes in elaborate ways. Grapes were kept fresh for months in closed sheds—each cluster with its stem immersed in a bottle of specially prepared water. Apples and other fruits were stored with impeccable care, as were vegetables. Special storage areas were prepared to accommodate the varying conditions needed to keep the different crops in prime condition during storage. This extravagant production of food was for the benefit of the members of the household and as many house guests as were invited to share in the bounty.

Today's kitchen garden is not such an elaborate affair, but you can recapture some of the elegance provided by such a garden. It must answer the same purpose as those in Victorian days, yet be scaled down to fit the size and time constraints of the modern family. This evolution of the kitchen garden is necessary, for it serves those who plant it with the many rewards the horticultural pursuits have to offer.

In this book are three practical kitchen garden plans designed with today's family in mind. Within these plans you will be able to customize and formulate your garden to reflect the type of garden you wish to have. The choice of plant material is yours to make and your plan must be adapted to fit your available gardening space. This book will also provide you with the horticultural basics, particularly those regarding soil, because understanding your soil is essential if you are to have good results.

Later chapters explore the components of the kitchen garden: vegetables, herbs, flowers, and fruits. A chapter dedicated to each of these elements includes specific cultural information. We will also explore old and new varieties of fruits, vegetables, and flowers that are especially garden-worthy. Finally, an extensive source list will speed you on your way to finding all the products and services you need to get started in your quest for the ultimate kitchen garden.

OPPOSITE: Traditionally, kitchen gardens often occupied tiny spaces such as the small plots outside a cottage or farmhouse. This city garden makes the most of available space by including plantings in containers.

kitchen garden basics

It never fails to amaze me how many people try to garden without having the slight-est idea what they are doing with respect to their soil. Without the foundation of good workable soil, a garden—and especially a kitchen garden—has only your good

intentions to grow on. Perhaps you think that soil is a mystery that cannot be unraveled, or that understanding soil requires a sophisticated understanding of chemistry. This is not the case. If you read the information in this chapter carefully, you will have a basic grasp of how soil works.

WHAT IS SOIL, ANYWAY? Soil is made up of inorganic and organic materials. The inorganic materials are primarily worn rock and stone or minerals. The organic materials—materials that were once living—are made up of decomposing plant and animal matter and the microbial organisms that help to break them down. Soil type depends on the exact proportions of these components.

All is at the ready on this back porch, which features storage space for tools and room for transplanting—a perfect setup for the enthusiastic kitchen gardener.

There are two types of inorganic particles that largely determine your soil type—sand and clay. The presence of sand or clay will greatly affect the porousness of your soil, its nutrient content, and the way it reacts when it is worked.

Sand is the larger of these two particles, and is quite visible to the naked eye. Sand particles are "unreactive," meaning that they are chemically unable to give off nutrients or bind with any nutrients that may exist in the soil. Sandy soils drain water away quickly, and the water carries nutrients with it when it goes, leaving behind a low-nutrient soil.

Clay particles are too small to see with the naked eye; in fact they cannot even be seen with most microscopes. Clay particles, unlike sand, are "reactive." They store and will give off nutrients and bond with nutrients that are put into the soil. Since water drains slowly through these compacted particles, clay soil is usually wet or damp but reasonably high in nutrients.

Because of their respective sizes, sand and clay particles directly affect soil porosity. Soil porosity is determined by the number of air pockets that are in the soil, the amount of organic material in the soil, and the degree of soil compaction. This determines how quickly the soil drains away excess water. The more air there is between particles of soil (organic matter adds many air pockets), the faster excess water drains away. Sandy soils, with their very large soil particles, tend to be porous, while clay soils do not.

Soil porosity is very important to the growth of plants. If the soil is overly porous, it will be dry and any nutrients you place in the soil can be quickly washed away. If the soil is too wet, microbial activity is slowed and the release of nutrients that are present in the soil becomes sluggish. What we all strive to create is garden soil that is fertile and friable, or

The three basic types of soil are loam, sand, and clay (left to right).

loamy. Unless you are blessed with such soil (a rarity indeed), the only way to attain it is through a program of slowly building the soil structure through organic amendments.

To fully understand how organic amendments modify the soil, you need to consider the changes these amendments make to soil structure and pH, a measurement of alkalinity or acidity in the soil. Measured on a scale of 0 to 14, a pH of 7 is considered neutral. Readings below 7 are considered acidic; readings above 7 are alkaline. Most garden plants are happy growing in soil that is between 6.5 and 7 on the pH scale.

A reading too far below 6 or above 8 on the pH scale is a warning signal that the soil will struggle to produce healthy garden plants, with few exceptions. Soil that is overly acidic binds up nutrients and will not release them so that they may be used by plants. Soil that is overly alkaline also inhibits plant growth.

Generally speaking, sandy soils tend to be acidic and clay soils tend to be alkaline. These are generalities, however, as localized factors can change the pH of the soil. You should plan to have your soil tested so that you have a general sense of where on this scale your soil registers. Knowing the pH of your soil will give you a starting point for planning your soil amendments. While the pH of the soil is important, adding organic matter to the soil can also make

a difference—it tends to moderate the pH toward a more neutral reading over time.

As you can see, neither sand nor clay is ideal. If you have sandy soil, you try to make it more like clay, and vice versa. Either can be made into wonderful garden soil. If you understand the basics of fertilizers and soil amendments, you can negate the undesirable tendencies of your soil and create wonderful gardens.

HOW DO FERTILIZERS AND AMENDMENTS AFFECT THE SOIL?

Fertilizers add nutrients to soil that plants can utilize. While plants do manufacture their own food, it is important that certain nutrients and minerals be present in the soil to help them carry out the process of photosynthesis. Without these nutrients, the plants will suffer various deficiencies.

The three most valuable nutrients for plants are nitrogen, phosphorous, and potassium. These are the nutrients in most chemical fertilizers. The proportions in which these nutrients occur in the fertilizer are represented by a percentage, called an N–P–K value. For example, 5–10–5, a commonly sold chemical fertilizer, contains 5 percent nitrogen, 10 percent phosphorous, and 5 percent potassium.

While these nutrients are important, I do not recommend that you add them to your soil via chemical fertilizers. The primary reason for this is quite basic: they will add nutrients, but they will do nothing to help build the structure of your soil. Truly healthy soil that will support a variety of plants comes with the addition of nutrients and minerals in the form of organic amendments that will improve your soil struc-

ture and porosity, as well as feed your plants slowly and evenly over a long period of time.

In addition to adding nitrogen, phosphorous, and potassium to your soil, there are many other important minerals and trace elements that are important for healthy plant growth. Fortunately, serious deficiencies in minerals and trace elements are fairly rare. When they do occur, they can usually be treated easily with organic soil amendments.

USING SOIL AMENDMENTS

Learning which organic soil amendments are best for your soil type is a key to becoming a good gardener. The choices are many, and some are more cost-effective than others. In the amendments you choose for your garden, you will have to achieve a balance between desired soil type, availability, budget, and personal choice. Let's take a closer look at some of these amendments and how they will benefit your soil.

Lime

Ground limestone has been used for many years in the garden, and most gardeners know that it will raise the pH of acidic soils. Lime is sold in two forms—finely ground or pelletized. Pelletized lime releases very little dust when it is spread. The form you choose to use is a matter of personal preference.

There are also two types of lime—calcic or dolomitic lime. The latter contains the trace element magnesium, and is preferable because magnesium is vital for healthy plants. Though not a fertilizer itself, lime acts as a fertilizer because it "unlocks" the nutrients in overly acidic soil, making them available for plant use. It also has an effect on the way soil reacts with water. When added to clay soils, lime makes the clay bind together to form larger particles. This produces soil that is more

porous, and water can drain away more quickly. In sandy soils, lime tends to hold the sand particles together, which has the effect of conserving moisture in the soil. In addition, recent studies indicate that the presence of calcium in the soil aids microbial activity, which means that organic matter breaks down more quickly.

Lime should be applied well in advance of the growing season, and is best turned under or applied to cultivated soil. It is a good practice to lime the garden in the autumn. If you are using lime and rock phosphate (which is added only every third or fourth year to augment phosphorus and trace elements as part of your amendment program), apply them at different times of the year—perhaps lime in autumn and rock phosphate in spring. Even though both of these amendments will raise the pH of the soil, a healthy dose of organic matter such as compost or peat added to the soil should keep the pH in balance.

Generally, lime can be applied at a rate of 50 pounds (22.7kg) of lime per 1,000 square feet (93m²) of garden. For more details on the best application rate of lime for the soil in your area, consult your local cooperative extension office.

Greensand (0–0–5)

Greensand looks like a dark, dense green sand, and can be a good way to augment trace elements in your soil when properly applied. It is sometimes call Jersey sand because it was mined from the ocean bottom off the New Jersey seacoast. Nearly every type of soil will benefit from this useful amendment.

By applying greensand to your soil, you can beef up most any trace element deficiency before it has a chance to show up in your garden. Greensand also has the ability to absorb many times its weight in water, a benefit to clay or sandy soils.

The application rate of greensand must be exact because it contains aluminum, which can be harmful in large amounts. The application rate that is safe for food production is ¼ pound (113g) of greensand per 3 square feet (.3m²). To help you correctly apply greensand, weigh ¼ pound (113g) of greensand on a postal scale. Place the greensand in a container that you can use as a scoop and level off the ¼ pound (113g) of greensand; next, mark the level of the greensand on the inside of the container with an indelible pen. Repeatedly fill the container to the mark with greensand and apply it to a 1 foot by 3 foot (30 to 90cm) area.

Bonemeal (4.0–21.0–.20)

Bonemeal's high phosphorous content helps promote flowering and fruiting for bulbs or flowering shrubs and plants. It is readily available in powdered form and is easy to apply—just sprinkle it on the soil and lightly cultivate it into the surface. Bonemeal also contains calcium and tends to raise the pH of the soil. Bonemeal is usually applied once yearly at a rate of about 10 pounds (4.5kg) per 100 square feet (9.3m²). Bonemeal may not be cost-effective if your gardens are large. If rock phosphate is available in your area, it is a less expensive alternative and a good substitute.

Rock Phosphate (0–32–0)

Rock phosphate is made of ground phosphate rock. By reading the N–P–K number, you can see that its high phosphorous content will work wonders for flower and fruit production. Aside from being high in phosphorous, rock phosphate contains large amounts of calcium and many trace elements.

Rock phosphate is a very long lasting additive, because it does not leach out of the soil. It is insoluble and remains in the soil until plants use it up. For this reason it need not be

This compost bin uses a layering technique that mixes the composted items, and then layers them on top of one another in wooden trays. They trays can be rotated as the mix breaks down, so that you always have compost ready, and always have space for fresh composting materials.

applied any more often than every four years. The application rate of rock phosphate is 10 pounds (4.5kg) per 100 square feet (9.3m²). Rock phosphate releases more quickly in acidic soils or if it is applied in conjunction with other organic material such as manure or compost. Apply rock phosphate at a different time of year than you apply lime because the alkalinity of lime will inhibit rock phosphate's release.

Rock phosphate is not always easy to find, but has become more widely available from garden centers in the last several years. If your garden center cannot order it for you, try ordering from a farm supply store.

Peat Moss and Peat Humus

Peat moss has been used for many years as a soil additive, and recently peat humus, a similar material, has reached the marketplace. Peat moss is compressed sphagnum and other material that has accumulated over hundreds of years, such as in a peat bog. Peat humus is similar but has a coarser texture. The main benefit of these two additives is the volume they add to the soil when they are worked in thoroughly. Greater volume means more air space in the soil, and this is a great benefit for clay soils.

Another attribute of peat moss and peat humus is that they soak up many times their weight in water. This helps hold moisture in sandy soils and helps keep water from seeping into air spaces in clay soils.

Peat moss and peat humus are both acidic in nature, and are often used to condition the soil for acid-loving plants. Make sure to mix peat moss or peat humus thoroughly into the soil whenever it is used. A 1-inch (2.5cm)=thick layer of peat per 4 inches (10cm) of soil tilled is a good rule of thumb.

Leaves, Shredded Leaves, and Leaf Mold

Leaves are one of nature's most wonderful gifts to the gardener—they are a great additive for the soil and, best of all, they are free.

Leaves may be added to the soil in three ways. Used whole, they may be tilled in or turned under the soil. If you have a leaf shredder, you can shred your leaves to use as a mulch that will slowly decompose into the soil. Finally, you can use leaves to make a leaf mold to add directly to the soil.

To make leaf mold, place shredded leaves in an enclosure made of chicken wire. Let them sit over the winter and turn them frequently during the next growing season. Slowly, the leaves will begin to break down into the deep brown, friable, loose material known to gardeners as leaf mold. By summer's end the mixture should be ready to apply, though the breakdown rate varies depending on temperature and moisture. Luckily, leaf mold can be applied at any time. Leaf mold can also be made with whole leaves, but the process will take much longer.

There is a misconception about using leaves in the garden because they are acidic. If a regular program of organic additives has been implemented in your garden, leaves will pose no threat at all. A program that includes lime, rock phosphate, or bonemeal will counter any acidic tendencies.

Composted Sawdust

Sawdust is another soil additive that may be free for the taking. It does wonders for soil because it adds tremendous volume. A local lumber mill or woodworker may be a regular source of sawdust for your garden.

Sawdust must be aged before it can be used in the garden. If you use it while it is fresh, it will cause a severe nitrogen deficiency in the soil. To avoid this problem, simply pile the sawdust in an out-of-the-way spot where the elements can work on it—right next to the compost bin is a good location. Leave the sawdust there for about three months, turning it two or three times. It will then be ready to use. To apply the sawdust, simply turn or till it under the soil.

Wood Ashes (0–1.5–7.0)

Wood ashes are especially helpful to root crops because the high percentage of potassium helps root development. In addition to this, the leaching action of a topdressing of wood ashes helps deter root crop pests such as root maggots. Many gardeners save them especially for use on crops such as carrots, parsnips, or beets.

Wood ashes are often available at no cost; those from a wood-burning stove or fireplace are fine for the garden. Wood ashes must be applied with care because they can burn your tender plants. To apply them to the garden, broadcast or top-dress around the plants, or they may be turned under with other additives. If you top-dress with wood ashes, be certain that the ashes themselves do not land on the leaves of the plants. Should this happen (or just to be on the safe side), water plants liberally with a hose after wood ashes are applied.

Apply wood ashes at a rate of 10 pounds (4.5kg) per 100 square feet (9.3m²). Avoid contact with your eyes and skin, and avoid breathing in the ashes as you sprinkle them or turn them under.

Compost

Compost is one of the most valuable additives for the kitchen garden, as all the waste from the garden is recycled back into the soil from which it came. Composting makes very good sense indeed.

The method you choose for composting is a personal decision. Some methods take more time than others, and some are quite labor-intensive. Composting is made easier if you have a shredder of some type that will increase the surface area of the material before it goes into the compost pile. This cuts down on the time it takes to make compost, and more importantly, cuts down on labor.

Some municipalities make compost available to their residents free of charge. Before using compost from these sources, call to be sure that items such as treated, stained, or painted wood, which may be toxic, are not being composted.

Compost is usually turned under into the soil. You may use as much as you like to improve your soil. Compost can also be top-dressed

around your plants during the growing season to give them an extra boost.

Grass Clippings (1.2–0.3–2.0)

Grass clippings are a fine additive for your garden, providing they meet certain requirements. Never use grass clippings in your garden if herbicides or pesticides have been applied to the grass within the past three months. The chemicals on treated grass clippings may be absorbed by your plants, which could be harmful to them or to you if you are eating produce from the garden.

Grass clippings are best tilled under the soil, but the time of year they are available makes this difficult unless an area of your garden lies fallow. Grass clippings can be composted, but a lot of other materials are necessary to help break them down, and after a few weeks there is usually too much grass for a good balance. Grass clippings can be used as mulch if they are not applied too thickly. If the grass is layered too thickly, and does not break down quickly enough, it becomes a fetid mess. Lastly, grass clippings can contain weed seed if your lawn is not weed-free. For all these reasons, they are best used with forethought. Often, the best place for grass clippings is on the lawn from whence they came.

Fresh or Composted Manure

Manure has long been a source of renewal for the garden. Years ago, barnyard animals served a secondary role as abundant producers of manure. Although it is not free for the taking, bagged, composted manure is easy for many gardeners to find and offers other advantages—it is ready to use and free of weed seed. The controlled heat from the composting process kills off most weed seeds. Since there are usually enough weed problems in the garden, we try not to import them deliberately.

On the other hand, if fresh manure is available to you and you are on a strict budget, you may decide to tolerate the inconvenience of having to compost it yourself. You should compost fresh manure for three or four months before you use it.

Manures vary widely in their nutrient values. Surprisingly, poultry and rabbit manures are the highest in nutrients. Any type of manure, though, will benefit your garden.

Composted manure can be applied to the garden in several ways. Tilling it in, if you have a tiller or cultivator, is best. It can also be turned in with a hand tool or may be top-dressed around your plants until the next time you till the garden.

CHOOSING AND PREPARING A SITE

Analyzing a site for your kitchen garden should be a simple task. For those of us with small city or suburban lots, there is usually not a great deal of choice about where to put the garden. It is important, however, to know what types of conditions your garden will require in order to thrive. The amount of available sunlight and the way you prepare the soil you before planting will make a big difference in the results you see from your garden.

LIGHT

The most important factor aside from the soil is the amount of light your plants will receive. In order to thrive, most vegetables, fruits, and herbs need lots of sunshine. "Full sun" means a minimum of six hours of direct sunlight each day. Eight hours or more of good strong sunlight will boost the productivity of your garden.

Morning light is much stronger than the fading light of day. If you have a choice between the two, there should be no hesitation—plant your garden in the spot with strong morning sun.

If you don't have a sunny location for your garden, you may need to adjust your idea of how many food-producing plants you will be able to grow. Perhaps you can find a full-sun location for a container of herbs or a trellis of runner beans and other vining vegetables, even if you don't have space in the sun for a full-scale kitchen garden.

DRAINAGE

Good drainage is among the most important growing conditions, but poor drainage can be improved. Given a choice, a nice gentle slope is the best site for most gardens, especially if the slope faces the south or east, allowing the garden to be warmed by the sun. Most of us, however, will have fairly flat ground.

A poorly drained site will have standing water during heavy rain. Adding any of the amendments discussed (see page 16) should improve drainage. If your soil is soggy beyond the help of amendments, you may opt to plant your garden in raised beds. Raised beds afford better drainage, and if your soil is likely to need several years of improving in order to reclaim its health, raised beds may save you time, aggravation, and money in the long run. If this is the case, you are better off "manufacturing" the soil in which you will be growing by filling your raised beds with quality topsoil that has been mixed to suit your crops (See more about constructing raised beds on page 27.)

PREPARING THE SITE FOR YOUR KITCHEN GARDEN

Preparing the site for the kitchen garden is pretty straightforward. First, all existing vegetation must be removed and then the soil should be dug and amended. Before you begin, you will want to lay out the plot on paper, in order to be sure that you clear enough land. (See Chapter 2: Designing the Edible Landscape for ideas on laying out your kitchen garden.)

LEFT, TOP: Double digging ensures a good start for your garden by breaking up and improving the deeper layers of soil, which are closest to plants' roots. **LEFT, BOTTOM:** Before planting, rake each bed until its surface is smooth, breaking up any stubborn clumps with the tines of the rake. This bed is nearly ready to accept seed or transplants. **ABOVE:** A small tiller or garden cultivator is helpful for turning under top-dressed amendments as the season progress, turning under spent crops, and maintaining pathways.

Removing Vegetation

This dreaded step of removing vegetation is well worth the effort it will take. By removing the existing plant growth, you will be removing a great deal of the weed problem for future years—especially the root systems of the more tenacious perennial weeds.

To complete this step you will need a good sharp garden spade, garden shovel, or edger. Any one of these tools will edge the sod adequately enough for you to remove it. Edge out a small area, about 3 feet (90cm) square, by cutting through the sod and into the soil below. Turn the sod over, exposing the roots to the sun and the air to dry. Continue in each area of your garden, exposing the roots of the sod, until all has been turned under.

Once all the sod has been turned it should be allowed to dry thoroughly. As it dries, shake the soil from the roots, allowing no roots to return to the soil. This step saves all the topsoil in the area and puts it back into the garden where it belongs. When this has been completed, the vegetation can be disposed of.

Working the Soil

There is one rule that must never be broken when you are working the soil for your kitchen garden: never work the soil when it is wet. Working and walking on wet soil will eventually damage the soil's structure. This is especially true if you have clay soil.

To determine whether the soil is dry enough to be workable, take a fist full of soil and squeeze it tightly. Release your grip—if the soil has made a tight ball in your hand, it is too wet to work with. If the soil makes a ball that is loose and falls apart, it is fine and can be worked.

Amending the Soil

Any amendments that you plan to use for the season can be added to the soil as you work it. Amendments will be that much more available to your plants if they are turned under, where the soil's microorganisms can break them

RIGHT, TOP: Direct-seeded crops such as these lettuce and radishes need thinning as they grow. A small pair of sharp scissors makes the task much easier. **RIGHT, BOTTOM:** These bean seedlings are well spaced; they're close enough to make the best use of garden space but far enough apart to prevent crowding.

down. Broadcast or rake the amendments across the soil surface evenly and proceed with turning the soil.

Double Digging or Tilling the Soil

A rototiller or garden cultivator is a very useful tool for effectively turning the soil year after year, but if this is your first garden on the current site, there is no substitute for double digging.

By double digging the beds in your kitchen garden, you accomplish several things: the soil will be loosened to a greater depth than a tiller can reach, so that plant roots can more easily penetrate; drainage is often greatly improved; and the soil is aerated to a great depth, allowing water and organic matter to eventually find their way into the subsoil.

To double dig a bed, use a short-handled spade or straight-tined garden fork. Dig down one spade's depth, removing the soil and setting it to one side. Continue to dig the trench in this way until you reach the end of the bed. Next, dig down another spade's depth in the same location, setting the soil aside but separate from the first layer. When you are finished you will have a trench the length of the garden bed and two piles of soil. Fork over the soil at the bottom of the trench to loosen it, then fill halfway with the pile of topsoil (from the first spade's depth you dug). Finally, finish filling the trench with the lower level of soil and rake to smooth the bed off.

Using a rototiller or a simple garden cultivator is effective when tilling the soil in spring and autumn. Regular tilling greatly benefits the aeration of the soil and helps put amendments directly into the soil where they can be broken down.

If your kitchen garden is an average backyard size, a small cultivator is all you really need. Spread your amendments over the surface of the soil and cultivate to the depth of the tines on the cultivator. Finish cultivating each garden bed, then rake it smooth. You are ready to plant.

SEEDING OUT OF DOORS

Planting seeds out of doors is not difficult if you pay attention to a few details. Most of the seeds sown directly in the garden can be sown in a single row, an old-fashioned way of planting. In recent years, intensive planting of smaller beds in the garden has become quite popular. These plantings are made in beds that are slightly raised with mounded soil. Planting in this manner allows you to improve only the soil of the growing beds, thus concentrating your efforts on a smaller area. The soil for pathways is left unimproved. A compromise between these two methods can be used for some crops by planting in double or triple rows. This way, you will maximize use of space while maintaining some order in the garden.

Planting seeds requires two steps—final preparation of the seedbed and sowing the seeds properly in the soil.

The seedbed is ready to prepare once you have double dug or tilled and amended your soil. Before you plant any seeds, the soil must be fine and even. Rake the soil out, breaking up any clumps with the tines of the rake. Smooth out the surface of the soil until it is fine and level. You are now ready to plant in rows or make beds for more intensive planting.

Planting in Rows

Refer to the layout plan for your kitchen garden that you devised earlier (see page 19). Mark out your first row with stakes and twine, keeping the twine taut and the row straight. Using your hoe, draw it down the row, creating a trench of the appropriate width and depth for the type of seed you are planting (see individual entries for spacing and note the recommended planting depth on the seed packet). When you have finished the trench, measure off the recommended spacing for the crop you are planting and mark the ends for the next row to be dug. Move the stakes and twine and make the next trench. Continue in this way until you have made all the rows you need.

Sowing the Seeds

Once your rows or trenches are made, you can go back and plant the seeds. Each type of seed requires different spacing. Some seeds can be sown close together, while others need a foot (30cm) between seeds. This information is generally included on the seed packet. Place the seeds in the trench at the recommended spacing, starting at one end and seeding the entire length of the row. With your hoe, go back over the raised soil left from making the trench and fill in the row, taking care to cover all the seed. Tamp the soil firmly over the seed with the back of the hoe.

Intensive Planting Beds

Intensive beds can be just the ticket for a small kitchen garden. Preparation of the seedbed is only done in the areas where these beds are to stand. To achieve this, mark the beds out with twine so you know where the amendments should be worked in, then prepare the seedbed as usual.

For attractively planted intensive beds, many gardeners raise them a bit. This is easily achieved by edging the outside border of each bed using a shovel. The soil that is removed is added to the bed. This technique leaves behind distinct paths that may be weeded with a hoe or mulched with the material of your choice.

Once the beds are edged, smooth them once again and you will be ready to plant. Trenches for planting in intensive beds are prepared as usual, and spacing of seed remains the same. However, because the amendments are concentrated, the rows are usually much closer together, making each bed wall-to-wall plants with no empty space between them.

Succession Planting

Succession planting has been practiced for generations in an effort to get the most from the investment in time and materials a garden requires. The idea behind succession planting is to follow a crop with a second crop as soon as the first is harvested. This allows the most production from your valuable garden space.

Succession planting works best in areas that have long growing seasons or with crops that mature quickly. Long-season plants like corn, cabbage, and vine crops usually dominate the space they occupy for the entire season. Early crops such as lettuce, radishes, peas, or dill can usually be followed by a planting of beans, Chinese cabbage, or another autumn crop, even in northern areas.

Knowledge of your climate and a bit of experimentation will help you determine which crops can be planted in succession in your area. Your local Cooperative Extension Service may also be of help in assessing the combination of crops that will work well for you.

After a crop is through bearing for the season, remove it and compost it or till it into a fallow area of the garden. Give a boost to the soil where a succession crop is to be planted by adding some compost or manure, working it into the soil well. This will ensure that the soil is replenished, because the first crop will have depleted it somewhat.

Crop Rotation

Crop rotation is exactly what it sounds like—crops are rotated to varying positions in the garden from year to year and never grown in the same location in successive years. The reasons for this practice are basic. Each crop feeds upon the soil in a different way. By rotating the crops the depletion of certain nutrients in the soil is spread more evenly and no one area is more heavily taxed than another.

Another reason for crop rotation is to prevent disease. Tomatoes, peppers, and potatoes in particular are prone to developing certain diseases if grown in the same spot over and over again. It is safe to plant a crop in the same location once every three years.

PESTS AND DISEASES IN THE GARDEN

Pests and diseases go hand in hand. Often, disease is spread by insects that feed and move from plant to plant. Pests are unavoidable in the garden, but you'll find that good garden practices such as autumn cleanup and preventive organic measures will help minimize problems. Common garden pests include aphids, leaf hoppers, cabbage worms, spider mites, white flies, and Japanese beetles. All but Japanese beetles can be controlled with organic sprays such as rotenone/pyrethrum, insecticidal soap, and BT (Bacillus thruringiensis). You can find these products at most large garden centers or through mail-order catalogs. Toxic chemical controls should never be used in the kitchen garden—after all, you will want to enjoy the fruits of your labor with a clear conscience. In order to use these organic sprays safely and effectively, you must understand how they work and how to best apply them.

Rotenone/Pyrethrum

Rotenone/pyrethrum is an organic insecticide combination spray that is more effective than pyrethrum alone. Both components of this spray are derived from plant material. This pesticide kills by paralyzing the insect, and so must be applied directly to them. It breaks down in about twenty-four hours when exposed to sunlight and so is only effective for one day. For this reason, food crops can be safely eaten a day or so after spraying with this compound.

Rotenone/pyrethrum is a broad spectrum organic insecticide, meaning that it will kill a wide variety of insects, both harmful and beneficial. To use this mix safely, you must be selective about its application in order to limit the damage to any beneficial insects that might have taken up residence in or near your garden. Apply pyrethrum/rotenone during daylight hours, spraying it directly on the plants. Avoid spraying flower heads, as this compound is deadly to pollinating honeybees. Never spray any pesticide when it is breezy or windy. The wind-carried pesticide can damage beneficial insects in nearby areas.

Insecticidal Soap

Insecticidal soap is a specially formulated soap for use in the garden. Its purpose is twofold: first, it acts as an adherent, helping spread and keep other pesticides on plant leaves, where they can be most effective. For this reason, it is recommended that you include insecticidal soap whenever you spray. Second, insecticidal soap coupled with the rays of the sun kills soft-bodied insects quite effectively.

Insecticidal soap is very safe for humans, but as with any other insecticide, it should never be sprayed in breezy or windy conditions because of the potential to damage beneficial insects in neighboring areas.

BT (Bacillus thuringiensis)

BT is a pesticide that affects only caterpillars. It works by interfering with a caterpillar's ability to digest food, but to be effective the caterpil-

lar must ingest it. BT is quick-acting, usually killing off caterpillars within an hour of being sprayed.

The cabbage butterfly, which lays its eggs on cabbage plants, is a problem in most areas of the country. The color of the caterpillar camouflages it perfectly, making this insect nearly impossible to see on cabbage, broccoli, and cauliflower. For this reason, it is advisable to spray your cabbage crops if you see this butterfly active in your garden.

The deadly action of BT is not lost on other types of caterpillars either, so be especially careful when applying it and make sure you are not doing so in breezy or windy conditions. This will no doubt affect local wild populations of monarchs and other butterflies.

Deer, Rabbits, and Rodents

This trio of pests is among the most maddening of garden problems. Deer and woodchucks are by far the most difficult to control once they learn that dinner is being served nightly in your backyard. They are brazen, forward, and difficult to control.

Rabbits inflict less damage. Whereas deer and woodchucks wipe out row after row of vegetation, rabbits pick at plants and hop to a new location. The damage perpetrated by rabbits is usually light and spread around enough to tolerate.

There are many products on the market meant to deter these critters. Many of these deterrents are available in spray form. Some make food crops inedible, so be sure to check the label. The disadvantage of these products is

Make sure that any pest controls you use in your kitchen garden are organic and safe. Any products applied to vegetables or herbs should be formulated for edible plants.

that rain lessens their effect and they will likely need to be reapplied. Even under the best of circumstances their performance is unpredictable—what works for one gardener will be ineffective for another and what works one year will not work the next.

In my experience, physical barriers are the best deterrent. Fencing placed over only the most vulnerable plants will stop the damage, but your dinner guests may help themselves to another item on the menu.

Fencing rabbits and woodchucks out of the entire plot is one solution. Occasionally, a rabbit will jump or squeeze through a fence or a woodchuck will burrow under it. These occurrences are easier to tolerate because they are more sporadic than the nightly raid.

Deer can jump fences over 8 feet (2.4m) in height. Electric fencing can do a good job of deterring deer, but check with local zoning officials, as it is sometimes not allowed in urban or suburban areas. In our rural area, electric fencing has worked well to date. Deer are creatures of habit—they receive an unpleasant jolt from the fence and change their grazing pattern to avoid getting a shock each night. Although they can jump this fence any time they want, they have not been so inclined, at least in our backyard.

Another product on the market to deter deer is known as "deer fencing"; it comes in several sizes and is made of long-lasting plastic mesh that is resistant to ultraviolet light. It would be nearly impossible for deer to walk through this type of fence, but unless it is quite high they can conceivably jump over it. The plastic that this fencing is made out of is black in color, so the fencing is difficult to see from a distance. The fact that this fencing does not impair the view and that it is undetectable makes it attractive to many gardeners who suffer with deer problems.

TOOLS

There are several tools that will make your chores in the kitchen garden much easier. Most are simple and can be found readily at local garden centers or through mail-order suppliers. When pricing tools, you will find a wide discrepancy. It has been my experience that a quality tool at a moderate price is usually the right choice. There is nothing more wasteful of time or more irritating than a tool that breaks in the middle of a job.

All hand tools should have a comfortable "feel" in the hand. Most garden catalogs are quite cognizant of the feel of the tools they carry, and take great pains to stock tools that are easy to use.

Taking good care of your hand tools will reward you many times over. Not only is it a waste to have to replace them often, but using a poorly maintained tool is annoying. The blade or area that comes in contact with the soil will need regular cleaning and care. Cleaning your tools at least annually—in late autumn, winter, or early spring—is essential. Rub all tool blades with steel wool pads to brush away the rust and sharpen any dulled edges with a metal file. Rinse the blades of your tools with a garden hose after each use, and wipe them with an oiled rag to keep the rust at bay.

Older brittle wooden tool handles can be conditioned with linseed oil each spring. Apply the oil with a soft cloth or with a small paintbrush. If the wood is thirsty, it will soak up the oil and you can apply again in another day or two. This treatment should make your tools' handles more supple and more resistant to moisture.

The hand tools described below are practical necessities for the kitchen garden. The power tools are strictly a luxury to save both time and hard labor.

The right tool for the job makes life much easier. This shed is well stocked with an assortment of forks, shovels, spades, weeders, and hand tools.

Trowels and Hand Cultivators

Trowels are similar to tiny shovels, and are most likely one of the oldest agricultural implements. They are necessary for so many

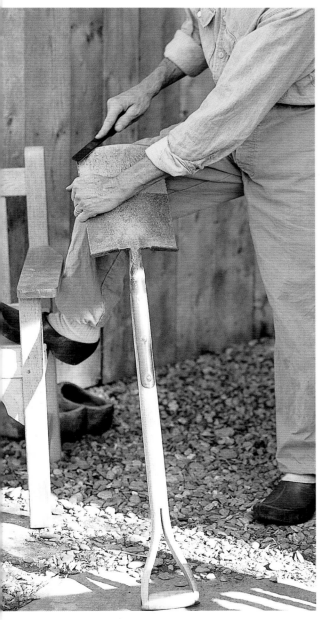

A file or sharpening tool helps keep garden tool edges sharp and free of rust, and ensures that the tools perform well every time they're used.

tasks in the garden that I can barely think of being without one. Trowels come in varying widths: narrower trowels are generally used for close confines and digging weed roots; the broader trowels are for more general excavating purposes.

Hand cultivators, which look like claws, and handheld hoes are quite useful for the odd weeding job when a regular hoe is just too large. They also can be used to cultivate amendments into the soil around more delicate plantings and for making narrow planting trenches. They are a must for any kitchen garden.

Similar to a handheld cultivator is a handheld hoe. These miniature hoes are great when you are on your hands and knees weeding. Their narrow blade enables them to get into a small space quite effectively.

Garden Shovels

A concave garden shovel that comes to a point is indispensable for digging large holes and for planting trees and shrubs. Shovels come with wood or fiberglass handles. Fiberglass-handled shovels are more expensive, but the handles last much longer than wooden ones. If you are prone to leaving your tools out in the rain, fiberglass is probably a better choice for you. When buying a shovel, pay attention particularly to the junction between the handle and the shovel itself. This spot is usually where breakage occurs, so make sure that the union is quite sturdy.

Garden Forks

A short-handled garden fork is even more versatile than a shovel. It has a square frame and straight tines, which bring to the surface every inch of the soil it disturbs. It is most useful for double digging and general loosening of the soil and for harvesting root crops.

Long-handled forks with rounded, slightly curved tines are used more for moving hay and like materials. A long-handled fork is a better tool for turning a compost pile than a short-handled fork.

Edgers

This simple long-handled tool—with its flat, semicircular blade—is a must for hand-edging your gardens. Used two or three times a year, it does a wonderful job of keeping the grass out of garden beds, and perhaps provides the simplest and most practical way of edging the garden. This tool can also be used for removing the vegetation from your proposed garden site and for edging your driveway and sidewalks. When purchasing an edger, make sure to choose one that has a sturdy joint between the handle and the metal blade.

Hoes

Hoes are useful for cultivating and weeding garden beds. A broad-bladed hoe is the most commonly used for these tasks. Hoes with narrower blades can be used in smaller areas or where many plants are grown close together. The hoe you purchase should have a sharp blade for "skulling" across the surface of the soil in pursuit of weeds. If the blade is dull, this skulling action will be more of a chore than it should be.

Garden Rakes

Two types of garden rake are commonly available. One is called a "T"-rake, the other a bow rake. The difference between the two is in the length and placement of the tines: T-rakes have short, straight tines, while bow rakes have longer, curved tines. Both are fine for smoothing the surface of the soil, but a bow rake's longer tines will cultivate more deeply in the soil, so it is generally preferred.

Cultivators and Rototillers

Cultivators and rototillers are not absolute necessities for a kitchen garden but they are useful, time-saving devices, and many gardeners would not think of gardening without

LEFT, TOP: Cold frames help tender house- or greenhouse-grown seedlings toughen up for the transition into the garden. The raised bed surrounding it offers additional growing space. **LEFT, BOTTOM:** Hand tools such as this garden claw are especially useful for cultivating around young seedlings and small plants. **ABOVE:** This small cold frame offers comfortable temporary housing for plants in transition or can be used to start seeds as the season progresses.

them. The main purposes of cultivators and rototillers are to aerate and break up the soil, to mix amendments into the soil, and to save time and manual labor, not to mention wear and tear on your back. The differences between a rototiller and a cultivator are mainly differences of size, power, and use.

Generally, rototillers are used to till large expanses of garden soil. They possess a great deal of power, dig deep into the earth, and can be used for a long time without taxing the engine.

Cultivators, as the name implies, are designed for a lighter workload. They do not dig as deeply as rototillers, cultivating only the top layers of soil. They are capable of mixing in amendments, and will aerate the soil. Cultivators are useful in small areas of the garden where a rototiller would be ungainly.

Note that tillers and cultivators are useless in perennial beds or near shrubs, fruit trees, or other permanent fixtures in the garden. The revolving tines will damage tender roots and have a negative effect on the plants.

The choice between a tiller or cultivator is a simple one. Tillers are readily available from rental services, and may be useful to fine-tune your kitchen garden beds in the beginning stages of their development. Unless you have a large area that will need tilling every year, a cultivator should do the job for you.

TEMPORARY AND PERMANENT GARDEN STRUCTURES

Traditionally, kitchen gardeners have made use of several structures that enable them to start their gardens earlier or help with the chores. Some are permanent structures and some are removable—examples include greenhouses, stone walls, and cold frames.

Gardening books and magazines are full of ideas that will help you plan and construct the more permanent features you want for your kitchen garden. Check the source list in this book to get started.

Greenhouses

Greenhouses serve a real need for the avid gardener. They provide a safe haven for tender plants in winter and act as a nursery for growing seedlings in the early spring. They may also be the only venue available for growing tropical plants, if that is your particular interest. Greenhouses require care and attention—even a small one requires dedication. To justify its cost and to fully recoup your investment, a greenhouse should be used in all seasons.

The average gardener will not need a greenhouse in order to manage a kitchen garden efficiently, but a cold frame is a near-necessity.

Cold frames

Similar in function to a greenhouse, a cold frame, as the name implies, is smaller and lower in temperature. A cold frame serves as a place where transplants can harden off (acclimate to a new temperature) and be partially protected from the effects of the sun, wind, and rain. If you are going to grow your own transplants, a cold frame will save you time, frustration, and failure.

Cold frames can be purchased via mail-order catalog. They can also be made from leftover or inexpensive building materials. Gardening magazines and local extension services frequently feature building plans for sturdy and inexpensive cold frames.

Whether you are purchasing a frame from a catalog or are building one yourself, there are some features you will want to be sure to allow for. The frame should be sturdy, and the building materials should be intended to withstand the elements. It should also be large enough to accommodate many trays of transplants.

Cold frames usually open with a large windowlike top that is attached at an angle. The angle makes good use of the sun's rays and allows rain to drain off instead of pooling up on the glass or plastic top. If you build the frame yourself, your plans should allow for the top to open partially. This is important because a closed cold frame can heat up during the day to dangerously high temperatures for the transplants. Many cold frames sold through catalogs have an opening device that is temperature sensitive. This prevents disasters if you forget to open the frame or are absent from your garden for a day or two.

Garden Walls and Fences

Garden walls add an elegance to the landscape that is unmatched, and, if tall enough, serve the purpose of keeping out animals and children. In times past, stone walls may have been erected in an effort to conserve heat, particularly in the spring and autumn months. The stones absorb heat by day, and release it into the surrounding air at night. Stone walls were also used to divide off sections of the garden, giving it a pleasing order. Time consuming to erect, stone walls are much more expensive and permanent than fencing, but if you can afford it, they will add a great deal to your landscape.

Fencing is comparatively inexpensive and thus is particularly valuable for today's garden. Placed behind the garden, a fence allows you to focus on and appreciate your garden by giving continuity to the background. An attractive fence can often add just the right touch to the back of a border or vegetable garden, and vining flowers or crops can be trellised along a fence, giving the structure double duty in the garden.

Beyond its aesthetic value, fencing can lessen the effect of wind on your garden and can be used to keep unwanted critters from invading.

Raised Beds

The value of raised beds for some kitchen gardeners can not be overstated. Those with impoverished soil or difficult-to-work clay will benefit greatly from the construction of raised beds for their garden. Though raised beds are a lot of work, they allow you to "manufacture" your own soil and grow a very nice garden indeed.

Make sure to construct raised beds for the kitchen garden with untreated lumber. You will be eating produce from the beds so you don't dare risk any chemicals leaching into the soil from treated wood. Heavy, untreated lumber is best, but it may be painted to provide some protection from rot.

When choosing plans for raised beds, be sure that they allow you to make adjustments for the size of the beds. Your raised beds should be no wider than 4 or 5 feet (1.2 or 1.5m) across, assuming the bed can be weeded from both sides. If the bed borders a wall, fence, or other structure, 2½ to 3 feet (75 to 90cm) is the maximum advisable width. The entire bed must be accessible for weeding, and this distance is a comfortable reach for most gardeners. The beds can be as long as you like.

A fine assortment of Chinese vegetables, including bok choy and mei quing choi, nears harvest time.

ABOVE LEFT: Raised beds are a good way to grow vegetables because they allow the most improvement to the soil. As a result of the rich soil, these rows of basil, lettuce, broccoli, and corn are lush and bountiful. ABOVE RIGHT: The frame for these row covers is permanently attached to the sides of the bed and will be completed with netting or garden fabric, ensuring protection for the plants within.

Many plans for raised beds show beds just 8 inches (20cm) deep, but to ensure good growth, plan for a minimum depth of one foot (30cm). If your budget allows, construct your beds at a depth of 15 inches (38cm), especially if your soil is exceptionally hard. Elevated beds, made without the help of wooden sides, are discussed on page 21.

Row Covers

Row covers are used to temporarily protect transplants of vegetables and flowers from strong sun, wind, or insects and animals. Once the row covers have served their purpose, they can be moved to another area of the garden or may be stored until they are needed again.

Row covers may be made of durable opaque plastic or lightweight fiberglass; they may also be made of a spun fiber similar to cheesecloth. Row covers made from more durable materials will last longer, but also take up more room in storage and are more expensive. Spun-fiber row covers last through a few

years of use if they are handled carefully and stored away after the season ends. If you are looking for protection from insect damage, spun-fiber row covers are the most effective. These row covers have the advantage of taking up little room in storage.

Row covers can be improvised and made at home from unused pieces of fencing, if your primary goal is to keep animals from grazing on your crops. Covers that will protect plants from the elements can be a little more difficult to improvise, so it is generally best to buy the ready-made covers if this is what you need.

KITCHEN GARDEN MAINTENANCE

When done on a timely basis, a few simple kitchen garden tasks will keep your plot healthy, productive, and attractive. Weeding, mulching, and path maintenance are the most time-consuming chores, but each is an important part of garden maintenance.

In the following section I have provided the basic what, when, and why of each garden

chore so that you get a better sense of the timing and importance of maintenance chores.

Mulching

Mulch is an important part of today's kitchen garden. Although it fell out of favor for a while after the introduction of chemical fertilizers, the use of mulch is back to stay. Gardeners have returned to mulching because it is organic and attractive, and cuts water use.

Mulching your garden has several benefits for both you and your soil or for the plants themselves. These benefits include keeping weeds down, conserving moisture, adding to the structure of the soil, and making the garden more pleasing to look at and work in.

The material you choose to use as mulch in your garden is a matter of personal choice, availability, and budget. Wood chips, pine bark, pine straw, shredded cedar, and shredded leaves can all make attractive and effective mulches. If you live in a coastal area, salt marsh hay may be available, and this makes a fine mulch. Barn hay is not as good a choice because it carries many weed seeds. Straw is a better choice than hay because it is composed mainly of plant stalks, but weed seeds may still be a concern.

Mulch is normally applied in the spring, once the soil has had a chance to warm up. The depth to which you layer the mulch in your garden depends on your budget and on the material you choose for mulching. Shredded leaves, wood chips, and pine straw can be applied several inches (centimeters) thick as long as they are not smothering plants in the process. Pine bark is not cost-effective to use more than an inch (centimeter) or so deep. Shredded cedar is very dense and can be applied thickly if it is not placed too close to the plants.

You may want to use one type of mulch for pathways and a different type of mulch in the beds themselves. Because they are more durable, wood chips and shredded cedar are good choices for mulching pathways. For vegetable and flower beds you may want to use a softer material such as shredded leaves. The leaves can be easily turned under at the end of the season and then replaced the following spring. A year or two of experience with these materials will help you decide which mulches work best in your area.

Maintaining Garden Paths

Unless you garden in a series of raised beds, paths will probably be a part of your kitchen garden. Paths allow for easy access to the growing beds and, if they are mulched, leave your shoes in a cleaner state than bare soil does. The drawback to paths is that they do require some maintenance in order to keep them looking neat and attractive.

Paths are easy to construct as you are laying out your garden. Once you decide where

LEFT, TOP: Starting seeds indoors is easy to do, and as a bonus, you'll have a much wider selection of plants available to you. LEFT, BOTTOM: These summer bedding plants have been transplanted into individual containers. Once they size up they will be easy to transplant. RIGHT, BOTTOM: Greenhouse shelves hold tray after tray of transplants and cuttings for the garden. Plastic greenhouse walls have been smartly insulated with a layer of bubble wrap.

you want your path to lead, outline all edges of the path with stakes and twine. If you will be growing in slightly elevated beds as described on page 21, edge out the beds first. Then, using your garden hoe, flatten the surface of the pathway. Any excess soil that is drawn up by the hoe can be put in the elevated bed. You are aiming for a flat, even path surface. If you are cultivating or double digging the adjoining beds, you will want to do so before the path is mulched for the season. Once the digging of the beds and the smoothing of the path is done, the path can be mulched with the material of your choice.

Since paths get a lot of foot traffic, the soil underneath becomes compacted. Even so, weeds can sprout along the edges. Some gardeners simply leave paths bare and weed periodically using a hoe. If your paths are mulched, an occasional weeding should keep them in good condition; if your paths are bare earth, expect to weed a bit more often.

Weeding

Weeding is one of the chores that most gardeners dread. As unpleasant as it is, weeding must be done on a regular basis because weeds in the garden rob your plants of necessary food and water.

You will encounter two types of weeds in your garden—annual weeds and perennial weeds. Some experience, observation, or advice from a fellow gardener will help you learn which weeds are annual and which are perennial.

Annual weeds are generally more easily destroyed than perennial weeds. They can usually be eliminated by occasional hand weeding or by weeding with a hoe. When using a hoe on annual weeds, the idea is to cut the stem of each weed. Once the stems are cut, the weed has little hope of survival. Some gardeners prefer to hand-weed, and smaller areas of the gar-

den call for this type of weeding. Hand weeding eliminates annual weeds by pulling them out root and all. When removing weeds from your garden, be sure to get to them before they set seed. This is especially important for annual weeds because they set thousands of seeds in a very short period of time.

When removing perennial weeds from your garden, it is essential to remove the entire root system. Any piece of root left in the soil can sprout another weed. Getting the entire root can be difficult because some weeds have extremely long roots, while others have roots that travel through the soil for quite a distance. Dig down the sides of the root to loosen soil and get as much of the root system as possible, then keep checking and removing any new growth that occurs. Although it is tempting to use a rototiller or cultivator on perennial weed problems, they will only make the situation worse by tearing the root system of the weed into tiny pieces that will grow back in time.

Watering

Unless you are having perfect summer weather, your kitchen garden will need additional watering. Vegetables, fruits, and annual flowers especially benefit from a steady 1-inch (2.5cm)-per-week rain or watering. Perennials and herbs require much less water, so you will need to water them less often.

When watering your garden, it is best to water deeply. Shallow watering only endangers your plants further as their roots turn upward toward the surface of the soil for the water they need to survive. Try watering weekly, soaking plants with 1 inch (2.5cm) of water all at once.

If you are unsure how much water your plants are getting, there is a simple way to find out. Take several small tin cans (they should have straight sides) and place them in the garden. The first can should be located a few feet

(meters) from the sprinkler, the second one should be an equal distance from the first, and so on until the last can is placed near the outer edge of the sprinkler's range. Water for an hour, and empty all the water collected in the cans into one large can. Measure the depth of the water by placing a ruler in the can, then divide the depth by the total number of cans. The final number you come up with is a good indicator of how much water your sprinkler is giving the plants per hour. Some simple math will tell you how long to water to achieve the ideal 1 inch (2.5cm) of water per week.

STARTING YOUR OWN VEGETABLE AND FLOWER SEEDLINGS

Raising your own seedlings for transplant has many advantages. If you can devote some time to it and have a little extra space in your basement, you can manage quite well. Raising plants from seed can be done inexpensively, even if you do not have a greenhouse or sunny window in which to grow them.

If you start your own seedlings, you will no longer have to depend on the varieties that local nurseries sell every spring. This is especially important if you live in an extreme climate—in regions with climatic challenges the exact variety you grow can make or break your season. Rarely do nurseries sell vegetable transplants designed to mature quickly in these short-season climates. You can beat the odds by growing transplants of your own choosing.

Materials

Starting your own seedlings requires only a small investment in materials, but you need to be sure that what you purchase meets certain requirements. Following you will find the essentials—good potting soil or soilless mix and serviceable growing containers—that you will need as well as details on their specifications.

SOIL Many types of soil and potting mixes are sold at garden centers. There is much confusion about which is best for growing seedlings or transplants. The best growing medium—and the choice of most professionals—is actually a soilless mix. This is specially designed for seedlings, and is light as a feather. Soilless mix is designed to absorb moisture and dry out relatively quickly, compared with potting soil. Wet soil may cause fungal problems for small seedlings, so the drier soilless mix is healthier for the little plants. There are several brands of soilless mixes sold across the country. The best test is to lift the bag—if it is light compared with "potting soil," it should be good for growing seedlings.

GROWING CONTAINERS Gone are the days when transplants were sown in shallow wooden flats. Today, plastic growing containers make growing seedlings much easier.

You'll often see recommendations that makeshift containers such as egg cartons make good inexpensive growing containers. My advice is not to waste your time on them; plastic "packs" are the only way to grow for both the novice and the experienced gardener. These plastic packs are inexpensive and reusable, and are widely available in different sizes to accommodate plants of varying vigor. Best of all, there is no shock or setback when they are transplanted. Instead of having to tear the root system and pry the seedlings apart, the entire root simply pops out of the cell and is ready to plant.

When choosing containers, keep in mind the vigor of the seedlings you will be growing and choose the size of the growing cells accordingly. The more vigorous the plant, the larger the cell should be in order to accommodate the root system until it is set in the garden.

Light

Most gardeners who start seedlings indoors need a supplemental light source. While you might think that you will be able to grow seedlings in a sunny window, this usually does not work out. Small seedlings need overhead light and lots of it. Those grown on windowsills are usually weak and spindly, and in the long run they do not measure up to those grown under artificial light.

The type of light source you use is a matter of budget and personal preference. There are all kinds of special light bulbs that are intended to reproduce sunlight—and there is much supporting literature that will tell you all the reasons you should be using these very expensive light bulbs. The simple truth is that all you really need to grow beautiful seedlings indoors is a simple, inexpensive fluorescent bulb.

Fluorescent bulbs are the next best thing to having a greenhouse. They are inexpensive to buy and use. There have no limitations in their use; they produce strong, healthy seedlings, and houseplants will even bloom under them.

One device that makes managing indoor lights easier is a timer. The timer can be set to give the seedlings the twelve to fourteen hours of light they need each day. This way, the lights will turn off on and off by themselves, and the seedlings will not suffer if you forget to turn them on.

Your setup for growing indoors need not be complicated or expensive. For many years I have grown seedlings under fluorescent lights successfully, and my setup is very simple. In the basement I have a 4-by-8 foot (1.2-by-2.4m) table made out of scrap lumber. Over the table I have strung what are commonly referred to as shop lights. Each one is 4 feet (1.2m) long and holds two fluorescent bulbs. Several of these shop lights will flood such a table with enough light to get the transplants off to a good start. Each one is on a chain so that the light can be moved up or down, depending on the height of the plants grown under it.

If you do not have a basement or if you desire a more aesthetically pleasing lighting arrangement, light tables of varying sizes are commonly sold through mail-order suppliers. This type of setup is attractive enough to be used in the main area of your home, and saves space by stacking several rows of plants one on top of the other.

When you first install each fluorescent bulb, it is a good idea to mark the date on one end of the bulb with an indelible pen. Fluorescent lights lose efficiency after one year and should then be replaced. Marking them with the date takes the guesswork out of when to replace the bulb.

Once your plants have germinated, keep the bulbs within 4 or 5 inches (10 or 12.5cm) of the seedlings. As the seedlings grow, the lights should be raised accordingly. Your plants will tell you if they are not getting enough light by stretching to reach toward it. This causes leggy, ragged plants, but can be corrected by bringing the lights closer.

Watering

Watering your tiny seedlings is a delicate task, and can be accomplished several ways. If you have trays to set the packs in, your seedlings can be soaked from underneath; the soil will take up moisture until it is saturated. This takes a fair amount of time if you have many plants. By far the easiest way to water is with a watering can that has a nice gentle flow that will not flatten the tender seedlings. A "rosette" on the end of the spout breaks the water up into a gentle flow. This type of can is available at garden centers or through mail-order suppliers.

Just how often you will have to water depends on the conditions in which your plants are growing. You do not want the plants to stay too wet, but if they dry out too much, they will die off quickly. Until you become accustomed to how often they need water, it is best to check them daily. Water them only when they need water, and then water them deeply. Do not water them again until they really need it.

Overwatering your plants and constantly surrounding them with overly damp soil can cause damping-off disease. This fungal disease usually kills seedlings quickly. It is characterized by seedlings that wilt for no apparent reason. Once this occurs, there is no remedy. If the soil shows evidence of a mold-like substance, but the plants themselves are not yet affected, place all affected seedlings in a dry, warm location to speed the drying of the soil. Sometimes a small fan will help hurry this along.

Fertilizing

Because your seedlings will be growing in a nearly sterile soil, they will need an outside source of nourishment. They should get one feeding every week with liquid kelp or a half-strength solution of houseplant fertilizer. A weekly feeding should be enough for your plants most of the time; but if their leaves begin to look a bit yellow, you may want to feed them a bit more often.

Planting

Many beginning gardeners jump the gun when starting seeds indoors. This is easy to do, especially if you have spring fever and live in a cold climate where the winter seems to drag on. Generally speaking, transplants should be started eight to twelve weeks before the last frost is expected in your area. The local cooperative extension service in your area will be able to help you if you are unsure when this is. Before making plans to plant, check the seed packet for the recommended timing on each variety, as some plants take longer than others to germinate and reach transplant stage.

Dampen the soilless mix with water a day or two before you intend to plant. This will keep dust to a minimum (you do not want to inhale a lot of dust from the peat in the mixture). Spread newspaper on your work surface.

Next, prepare the packs. You will notice slits in the bottom of each growing cell in the packs. These allow water to be taken up, but they can also allow soil out, so they need to be plugged. Cut small squares of newspaper to size, dampen them with water, and place a square in the bottom of each of the growing cells. Prepare all the packs you intend to plant so that they may be filled with soil.

Using a can or plastic mug, dip out the soilless mix and begin to fill the packs. You want them to be filled to the top because the soil will settle after the packs are watered thoroughly. Fill each pack with soil and place another pack on top of it, pressing down firmly. The soilless mix should be firm, but not compacted in each flat.

Before sowing the seeds, consult the seed packet. Seeds sold through reputable nurseries have sowing instructions included on the packet. These instructions will tell you how deeply to cover the seed and the preferred temperature for good germination.

Some flower seeds are quite tricky to germinate. Pay special attention to these instructions, which may include giving the seed total darkness or providing a lower temperature than is usually found in the home. Following these instructions to the letter will make all the difference; if you do not follow them, you are likely to get no germination at all. Generally, it is best to put more than one seed in each growing cell. This will save you the time of having to resow if some seeds do not come up. Most vegetable seeds germinate at a rate of about 80 percent, so don't expect that all the seeds will germinate even under the best conditions.

To water the grow packs, place them in a sink filled with lukewarm water. Be sure that the water is not so deep that it tips over the flats. Next, spray the top of the soil with a gentle mist from a handheld spray bottle until the soil on top is damp. This will help cut the time it takes to saturate the soil by half. Place the grow packs in a warm place (or in any special location or conditions indicated on the seed packet).

Germination time varies widely from plant to plant. Most vegetable plants will germinate in about one week, but many flowers take longer than this.

Transplanting Seedlings Outdoors

As the season progresses and the date of last frost nears, you should begin thinking about moving your plants to a transitional area so that they can "harden off" to outdoor conditions before they actually go into the ground. This is a necessary step because the transplants you grow indoors are quite tender. They have not been toughened by the wind or rain, nor are they used to the increasingly harsh rays of the sun or cool night temperatures. Putting them directly into the garden would mean certain death.

The exact timing of this hardening off period depends on your climate and circumstances. If you have a cold frame to protect them from the wind and cold, they can go outdoors as soon as nighttime temperatures will not freeze them (40°F [4.5°C] is warm enough for most seedlings except real heat lovers). If you do not have a cold frame, you may find yourself moving your transplants out during the day and in again at night until the weather is reliably warm enough for them.

Even if you have a cold frame, your transplants will probably need protection from the sun. Without this protection the plants will "bleach out," a condition like a severe burn. The leaves turn white and often the plants will die. The best way to guard them is with a screen; a simple recycled window screen will do the trick. Begin by keeping the screen over the plants all day, then reduce the hours gradually. After about ten days you should be able to leave the screens off except from about 11:30 A.M. to 1:30 P.M.; during these hours the sun is particularly strong. Gradually wean the seedlings away from all protection from the sun. Sometimes this can be helped along by a cloudy period of weather when the protective screen can be removed completely. Wind is also a concern when moving seedlings outside. They can easily be flattened by a gust, and if the stem is damaged the plant may never recover. Keep transplants covered in windy weather and expose them to breezes gradually. The exposure will help the stems strengthen. The same is true of rain, as a pelting rain can kill tender plants. Gradual exposure to a harsher spray of water from the garden hose will help toughen your transplants.

Young pepper and eggplant transplants grow to size in elevated beds with a colorful backdrop of zinnias, cosmos, and tickseed.

Chapter 2

designing the edible landscape

In order to lay out your garden, you first need to plan it on paper. You must figure out what you want to plant and where in the garden it will go. Take accurate measurements of your garden site, and draw a scale plan on graph paper. In the following pages you will find some ready-made garden plans that you can modify for your situation. Such plans are especially helpful for the beginning gardener.

If you are drawing up your own plan, consult the entries in the following chapters on the plants you wish to grow to learn how you should space the plants. Also note that most food-producing plants benefit from rows planted north to south, in order to make the most of available sunlight.

Mark with stakes the corners of the beds that need to be turned over. You'll also need to stake curved edges at several points along the edge. Connect all the stakes with sturdy twine to help you keep on target as you remove the vegetation and prepare the bed. Once all the areas are marked in this fashion, you are ready to proceed.

This charming plot is planted in a classic cottage style, with mixed herbs, flowers, and vegetables of all heights and hues. The rustic fence and stone-bordered pathways add to the country feel of this instensively planted garden.

A ROTATING vegetable plot

This plan is for someone who likes simplicity of design or wants to grow mainly vegetables. The plan may be implemented at ground level or may be composed of a series of raised beds.

Annual crops are intended to be rotated from bed to bed each year, so the beds are of a uniform size except for the pole bean and asparagus beds.

A main path through the center of the garden, plus wide paths along both sides and narrower paths between beds, allows complete access to each bed. Paths can be made of packed soil or can be mulched.

A permanent planting of asparagus (a perennial) at one end of the bed grows quickly into a lush background after the cutting season. Sturdy, permanent garden fencing flanks the garden. Grow peas on one side and follow them with summer plantings of bush beans or cole crops. The other side can feature cucumbers, melons, small winter squashes, and mini-pumpkins, all trained to the fencing to save precious garden space.

Rotate the crops in this plan each year to keep the soil enriched. Note that this plan is easily expandable, and can be adapted to accommodate more garden beds if desired.

SUGGESTED PLANTS:

1. Peas (thickly planted)
2. Pole beans
3. Tomatoes
4. Peppers
5. Carrots
6. Beets
7. Scallions
8. Swiss chard
9. Lettuce and salad greens
10. Radishes
11. Parsnips
12. Leeks
13. Onions
14. Cucumbers
15. Melons
16. Squash
17. Asparagus
18. Privet hedge

KEYSTONE PLANTS FOR THIS GARDEN:

While you can use any varieties you like, the following are particularly recommended for their beauty and dependibility.

'Joseph's Coat' Swiss chard

'Brandywine' tomato

'Romano' pole bean

'Ace' pepper

'Jersey' leek

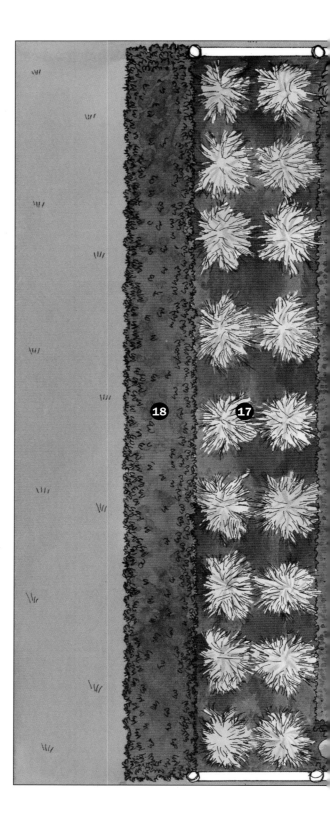

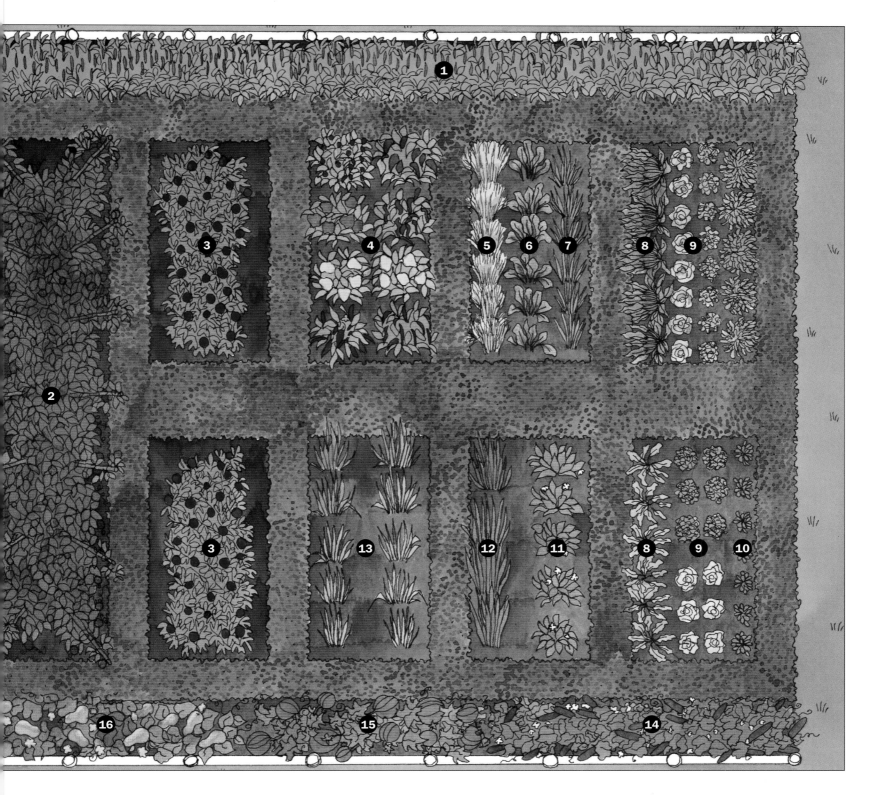

A TRADITIONAL
kitchen garden

This plan is fairly elaborate, and will take time and care to execute. The garden accommodates many different crops, and is designed to emphasize diversity. A visual delight, this design rewards the gardener as he or she works—from every vantage point there is something to enjoy.

At one end of the garden fruit trees and berry bushes create an enclosed space in which the gardener can find refuge all season. The bench situated there looks out at the focal point of the garden, a fountain placed squarely in the center. Bird baths and bee skeps placed near the bench promise to draw plenty of wildlife for the gardener to observe while relaxing. Stone seats at the sides of the garden also enjoy a view of the fountain.

The other half of the garden is a production area for greens and fresh vegetables, and features flowers, herbs, and fruits as well. The garden is laid out so that a variety of crops can be grown, rotating them between beds from year to year.

Maintain the paths as grass or packed soil. For a more formal look, lay gravel instead. A stone or brick wall adds visually to the garden and creates a feeling of separation from the rest of the landscape, but a decorative fence also works well.

SUGGESTED PLANTS:

1. Dwarf fruit tree
2. Currants
3. Gooseberries
4. Perennial flowers
   Autumn-blooming sedum (*Sedum spectabile*)—recommended cultivars: 'Autumn Joy', 'Vera Jameson'
   Coral bells (*Heuchera* spp.)—recommended cultivar: 'Purple Palace'
   Gayfeather (*Liatris spicata*)
   Lady's mantle (*Alchemilla mollis*)
   Painted daisy (*Chrysanthemum coccineum*)
   Purple coneflower (*Echinacea purpurea*)
   Snow-in-summer (*Cerastium tomentosum*)
   Wild bleeding heart (*Dicentra eximia*)
   Yarrow (*Achillea filpendula*)—recommended cultivars: 'Moonshine', 'Coronation Gold'
5. Perennial herbs
   Bronze fennel (*Foeniculum vulgare nigra*)
   Chives (*Allium schoenoprasum*)
   Lavender (*Lavendula angustifolia*)
   Sweet cicely (*Myrrhis odorata*)
   Winter savory (*Satureja montana*)
6. Tea garden
   Angelica (*Angelica archangelica*)
   Anise (*Pimpinella anisum*)
   Anise hyssop (*Agastache foeniculum*)
   Applemint (*Mentha suarcolens*)—container only
   Blue blasam tea mint (*Mentha* spp.)—container only
   Lemon verbena (*Aloysia triphylla*)
   Lemongrass (*Cymbogon citratus*)
   Scented geranium (*Pelargonium* spp.)
7. Swiss chard
8. Onions
9. Leeks
10. Carrots
11. Strawberries
12. Annual herbs
    Mexican basil (*Ocimum basilicum*)
    'Spicy Globe' basil (*Ocimum basilicum* 'Spicy Globe')
    Summer savory (*Satureja hortensis*)
    Sweet basil (*Ocimum basilicum*)
    Triple curled parsley (*Petroselinum crispum*)
13. Bush beans
14. Lettuce
15. Salad greens
16. Annual cutting flowers
    Dwarf sunflower (*Helianthus annuus*, dwarf cultivars)
    Garden balsam (*Impatiens balsamina*)
    Nicotiana (*Nicotiana* spp.)
    Snapdragon (*Antirrhinum majus*)
    Stocks (*Matthiola* spp.)
    Sweet William (*Dianthus barbatus*)
    Zinnia (*Zinnia* spp.)
17. Blueberries

KEYSTONE PLANTS FOR THIS GARDEN:

The following plants provide subtle color and substance in the garden.

Purple coneflower *(Echinacea purpurea)*

'Jean Davis' lavender *(Lavendula angustifolia* 'Jean Davis')

Anise hyssop *(Agastache foeniculum)*

'Music Box' dwarf sunflower *(Helianthus* 'Music Box')

'Only the Lonely' flowering tobacco *(Nicotiana sylvestris* 'Only the Lonely')

Mesclun mixed salad greens

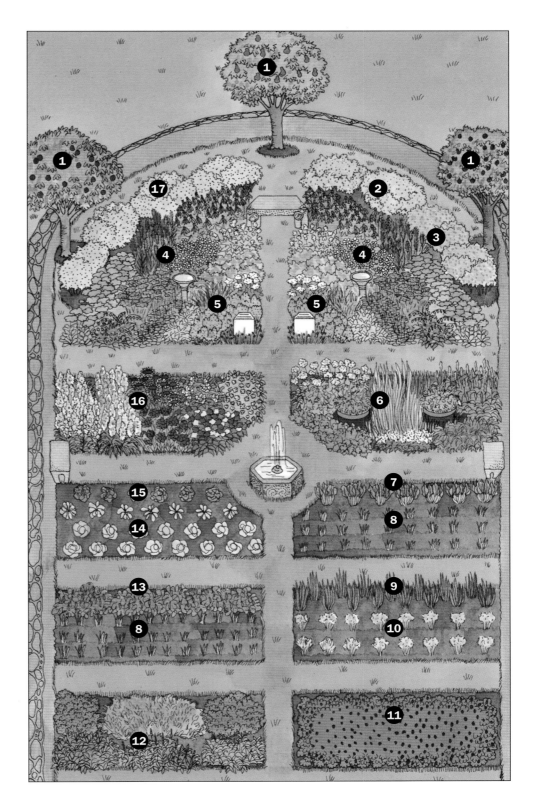

A COTTAGE-STYLE kitchen garden

A cottage-style kitchen garden is an expression of individual taste, and each cottage garden should reflect the personality of the gardener in charge. This plan, however, offers guidance for beginners and design ideas for more experienced gardeners in creating this lovely garden style.

This Cottage-Style Kitchen Garden combines fruit trees, bushes, flowers, herbs, and vegetables in mixed beds. The outer part of the garden contains many perennial plants and so is more permanent than the center, which features vegetables and annual herbs that should be rotated from season to season.

Old-fashioned tree hydrangeas and miniature roses—both of which are perfect for drying—bring a touch of nostalgia to the cottage garden setting. Everlasting flowers, too, are decorative in the garden and can be dried and used in arrangements long after the gardening season is over.

The rock garden at the entrance to the garden creates a pleasant view from home and from the stone seat. Located next to the water garden, the stone seat provides refuge and is tucked away from the prevailing view of the garden. The relaxing sound of running water adds a cooling sense to this restful area.

Paths allow access to the entire garden. They may be made of packed soil or may be mulched.

SUGGESTED PLANTS:

1. Dwarf fruit tree
2. Currants
3. Perennials and everlasting flowers
   Rose campion (*Lychnis coronaria*)
   Baby's breath (*Gypsophila paniculata*)
   Yarrow (*Achillea filipendula*)
   Globe amaranth (*Gomphrena* spp.)
   'Bikini' strawflower (*Helichrsyum* 'Bikini')
   Love-in-a-mist (*Nigella dmascena*)
   Sweet Annie (*Artemisia annua*)
   Annual statice (*Limonium sinuatum*)
4. Miniature roses (*Rosa* spp., miniature cultivars)
5. Hollyhocks (*Alcea rosea*)
6. Onions
7. Eggplants
8. Peppers
9. Ornamental kale
10. Filbert tree
11. Rock garden
    'Tiny Rubies' pinks (*Dianthus* 'Tiny Rubies')
    Mountain avens (*Dryas octopetala*)
    Snow-in-summer (*Cerastium tomentosum*)
    Hens and chickens (*Sempervivum* spp.)
    Siberian draba (*Draba sibirica*)
    Flower of Jove (*Lychnis flos-jovis*)
    Rock cress (*Arabis fernandi-coburgi*)
    Pink (*Dianthus gallicus*)
    Pink (*Dianthus arenarius*)
    Tussock bellflower (*Campanula carpatica*)
    Sea thrift (*Armeria maritima*)
12. Cherry tomatoes
13. Bush beans
14. Ruby chard
15. Lettuce and other salad greens
16. Scallions
17. Radishes
18. Tea garden
    Lemon balm (*Melissa officinalis*)
    Chamomile (*Chamaemelum nobile*)
    Pineapple sage (*Salvia elegans*)
    Bergamot mint (*Mentha* spp.)—container only
    Scented geraniums (*Pelargonium* spp.)
19. Annual herbs
    Anise (*Pimpinella anisum*)
    'Purple Ruffles' basil (*Ocimum basilicum* 'Purple Ruffles')
    Italian parsley (*Peroselinum* spp.)
    Savory (*Satureja hortensis*)
20. Hydrangea (*Hydrangea* spp.)
21. Siberian iris (*Iris sibirica*)
22. Dwarf Alberta spruce (*Picea glauca*)
23. Blueberries
24. Coral bells (*Heuchera* spp.)
25. Hostas (*Hosta* spp.)
26. Peonies (*Paeonia* spp.)
27. Clematis (*Clematis* spp.)
28. Queen of the meadow (*Filipendula ulmaria*)
29. Bronze fennel (*Foeniculum vulgare nigra*)
30. Asiatic lilies (*Lilium* hybrids)
31. Heart-leaved bergenia (*Bergenia cordifolia*)

KEYSTONE PLANTS FOR THIS GARDEN:

These cottage garden plants marry function, beauty and tradition.

'White Imperial' currant

'Pretty in Purple' and 'Lipstick' peppers

'Buttercrunch' lettuce

Bronze fennel *(Foeniculum vulgare nigra)*

'Sweet Gold' cherry tomato

outstanding vegetables

The vegetable patch is heaven for many gardeners and is certainly the heart and soul of the kitchen garden. Not only can you create a beautiful garden you can enjoy, but the fresh produce you grow will be the star of the evening meal.

Deciding which vegetables you want to grow is simply a matter of personal taste. There is no sense in laboring to produce vegetables that you or your loved ones are not fond of. No matter the climate, there is an extensive list of favorite vegetables that are easy for the average gardener to grow. These popular vegetables are the focus of this chapter.

The vegetables you grow will either be directly seeded in the garden or they will be grown from seedlings. Direct-seeded vegetables need thinning and additional care until they mature to the size of substantial seedlings. Vegetables from transplants need little care once they are established in the garden; they'll survive with just regular weeding and watering like the rest of the garden.

Edible strawberries intermingle with chives, lettuce, and ornamentals in this corner of an intensively planted bed.

Consult Chapter 1: Kitchen Garden Basics for information on direct seeding and starting from seed. The vegetable plots in the kitchen garden can look rather dull in the early part of the growing season, but this is more of a problem in northern areas. This is to be expected, however, and there is little to be done about it. If the look of the early-season vegetable garden bothers you particularly, fence the plots or integrate them into other areas of the garden. When combined with patches of growing plants, the vegetables' deficiencies will not be as evident as if they had their own expanse of garden. Once the vegetables have grown in they will be beautiful, though harvest will take a necessary toll on aesthetics.

INTENSIVE PLANTING

Vegetables in the kitchen garden may be intensively planted (see page 21) whenever it is practical. Not all vegetables can be planted in this way, but crops such as beets, carrots, and salad greens are perfect for this technique.

Intensive planting of vegetables in the kitchen garden serves many purposes. You'll save space when carrots, for example, are planted in triple or quadruple rows instead of single rows. When you plant in this way, you need not provide space for a path between each row. If you plant intensively, you will need to plan for a bed that is no wider than 3 feet (90cm) across, so that the center of each bed can be accessed from the sides.

Intensive planting also makes the best possible use of the soil you have so carefully prepared. If you have been diligent in your soil preparation, the yield per square foot should top that derived from traditionally planted crops. Amendments are not wasted on path areas but are put only where they are needed.

The space and labor saved by not preparing additional garden soil for the paths is con-

siderable. Lastly, intensively planted beds look more ornamental than their traditional counterparts because more greenery than soil shows. A plot of densely growing salad greens, with varied leaf textures and colors, looks wonderful in its prime.

Intensive planting is not for every crop. Some plants are just too large, feed too heavily on the soil, or are too susceptible to disease if crowded. For these crops I have suggested alternative space-saving techniques where appropriate.

VEGETABLE PESTS

SLUGS

Slugs are tough little creatures that are not very appealing to look at and can do a lot of dam-

age in the garden. They are somewhat nocturnal and have a tendency to hide under boards and other objects in the garden during the day.

Slugs are difficult to control, partly because pesticides aimed at slugs are pretty heavy hitters and are not something you want in your soil. Of the slug-control methods availabe, none work well for everyone, so dealing with these pests is largely a matter of trial and error. Following are suggestions that may help you control slugs, if you find they are attacking your garden.

- Place shallow bowls of beer in the garden. Slugs love it and will drown before they can get out of the bowl.
- Place boards in the garden on the ground or just a bit above ground level. Check in the

---

Seed Buying Information and Viability

When buying vegetable seeds, or any seeds, it is easy to go overboard. Ideally, you want to keep the amount of seed you have on hand in check; you should have enough to get through the year, but that is all. The reason is that many seeds need to be purchased fresh each year—after a year they lose viability and will not germinate well. Exceptions are noted in the chart below. Corn and bean seeds are more cost-effective to buy in bulk, and since the seeds will keep, most gardeners take that approach. Do keep in mind that while the seeds kept over may germinate, the rate will not be the same. You will have to plant more seeds to get good germination the second year.

Seeds that should be used in the first year:	Seeds that can be saved through a second year:
Onion	Cole crops
Leek	Swiss chard
Lettuce and salad greens	Beet
Parsnip	Bean
Pepper	Corn
Eggplant	Cucumber
Pea	Melon
Carrot	Summer squash
	Winter squash
	Tomato

morning for slugs hiding underneath. Destroy any slugs you find.

• Place copper strips around the plants that slugs love. The theory is that the slime secreted by the slugs reacts with the copper and electrocutes the slugs.

• Sprinkle salt on any slugs you find, which will dry them up, killing them in the process.

• Buy a small box of slug bait, but do not put the bait directly in the garden. Instead, put a small amount in a recycled plastic container and moisten the bait slightly. Place the container near problem areas by digging it into the ground so that the top is even with the surface of the soil. Place a pot over the open end of the container, bracing it on a rock so that slugs can still get to the bait. Put a rock on top of the pot so that the wind can't blow off the cover—this will prevent birds and other small mammals from getting into the slug bait.

The bait can be renewed every three weeks or so, and the entire trap can be disposed of at the end of the season. This method prevents the slug bait from entering your soil and eventually your plants.

CUTWORMS

Cutworms are sizable grubs that inhabit the soil in many gardens. They get their name because of the manner in which they feed. At night they emerge from the soil, chew the stem of a seedling in half, and eat the spoils. The next morning there are short stubs left where you once had transplants.

Cutworms are pretty easy to outsmart by encircling your transplants with a collar. This prevents the cutworm from getting to the tender stem. Also, you should be looking for cutworms when your transplants go into the soil, destroying any you find. If you miss them, they can come up inside the collar and still destroy your plants.

Cutworm collars are easily made by taking the top and bottom off a regular tin can—tuna cans work great, but others can be used for this job too. The cans are durable and will not be damaged by the elements, lasting for many years.

VEGETABLE VARIETIES

The number of named varieties of each vegetable can be a bit staggering to the beginner. Over the years, nursery growers have been developing vegetables for better flavor, higher yield, and adaptability to growing requirements.

While flavor can be a matter of personal taste, yield is objective. Hybrids have been developed because, in general, they outperform the older open-pollinated varieties under normal conditions. Even so, over the last few years there has been a renewed interest in "heirloom" vegetable varieties. Many gardeners compromise, growing a mix of the old and the new, until they find those varieties that do best in their own gardens. In Sources, on page 132, you will find suppliers that specialize in the seeds of heirloom varieties, as well as many companies that offer new introductions.

If you live in an extreme climate with a short growing season, not enough can be said about the varieties of vegetables you choose for your garden. Many varieties suitable for long growing seasons will not do well under adverse weather conditions, and planting these in your kitchen garden can result in a lost season. Take time to study the catalogs and do your best to select varieties that are suited to your climate and your growing conditions. If you are planning to grow vegetables such as tomatoes and peppers from seedlings, this advice is especially important. Do not depend on garden centers to choose the correct varieties for your area. Again, refer to the source guide, as seed sellers

that specialize in providing seeds for extreme climates have been listed and called to your attention.

The following pages are devoted to the most popular vegetables for the kitchen garden. For each vegetable listed you will find tips on growing and spacing the crop.

ASPARAGUS

Asparagus is unusual among vegetables because it is a perennial that can be harvested year after year. The young shoots, or spears, as they are called, are cut off just below ground level before the leaves open. After the cutting season, asparagus develops attractive fernlike leaves 4 feet (1.2m) high or more. Asparagus can make a nice background for the garden all summer long.

Asparagus is usually planted from purchased roots, but can also be planted from seed. The newer all-male varieties are said to yield as much as two to three times that of regular asparagus (female plants put much of their energy into producing flowers and seed). Asparagus is planted in the spring and allowed to grow for a full season before it is cut for harvest the following spring. The first full year, you can cut the earliest shoots, and thereafter you can cut shoots during the regular season. In northern areas, the cutting of asparagus is over by the Fourth of July.

To plant the roots, dig a hole at least 12 inches (30cm) deep and wide enough to fit the roots with room to spare. Fill the bottom 6 inches (15cm) of the hole with compost or composted manure. Make a mound in the bottom of the hole and set the root on top of the mound, the roots trailing to the sides. The root crown should be 4 to 6 inches (10 to 15cm) below ground level. Place 1 or 2 inches (2.5 to 5cm) of soil over the roots. As the asparagus shoots begin to grow up, fill in each hole.

Planting holes should be spaced 18 inches (45cm) apart.

If asparagus beetles are a problem in your area, be sure to take away the asparagus foliage at the end of each year and dispose of it or burn it—do not compost it. Eggs can overwinter in the old foliage (or even the mulch), so if they persist you may want to rake off the mulch early in the year and replace it in mid-summer.

There is no way to save space when planting asparagus, but unless you want a large bed, you may consider working it into the back of a perennial border or kitchen garden.

BEANS—BUSH BEANS, SHELL BEANS, AND POLE BEANS

Beans are one of the most prolific and easiest vegetables to grow. Bush "stringless" beans and shell beans are grown in the same fashion, but pole beans require supports on which to grow.

All beans are legumes, and benefit from the use of inoculant (a beneficial natural bacteria that helps the germination rate and general growth of the plants) on the seeds before they are sown. Inoculant looks like a black powder and is mixed into the dampened seed before planting. Legumes also fix nitrogen in the soil, a benefit to those crops grown in their space the following season. Many gardeners make a habit of following beans with a heavy-feeding crop the next season.

Do not plant bean seed before the soil has warmed to a temperature of about 65 degrees.

RIGHT: Picking asparagus fresh from the garden is a true pleasure of spring. OPPOSITE, TOP: Scarlet runner beans are a cool-season pole bean variety grown for either their edible pods or colorful dried inner beans. As a bonus, the flowers are a bright scarlet red, and a favorite of hummingbirds. OPPOSITE, BOTTOM: This orderly kitchen garden bed includes young pumpkin vines, dwarf sunflowers, and nasturtiums, as well as two varieties of cabbage.

This usually coincides with the last expected frost. Bean seedlings are very sensitive to cold, and seed planted in cold soil will often rot. Bean seed should be planted in drills (small trenches) made with a hoe that are 1 to 2 inches (2.5 to 5cm) deep. Space the seeds 2 inches (5cm) apart in the drill and space the rows about 18 inches (45cm) apart. This will leave room for air circulation between plants and lessen the chances of disease, which is encouraged by wet conditions. Pole beans can be trained up poles, netting, or trellising in the garden, thereby saving space. Pole beans have a fuller, more robust flavor that many people prefer.

Most varieties of bush beans and pole beans mature in about 55 to 65 days. Bush beans can be planted in waves two weeks apart so that there is always a fresh crop in the garden. Pole beans will continue to produce all season. Shell beans are a long-season crop and most have a maturity period of about 90 days. They are harvested when the pods are dry and the beans rattle inside.

CABBAGE, CAULIFLOWER, AND BROCCOLI

Cabbage, cauliflower, and broccoli, referred to as cole crops, are all related and they have similar cultivation requirements. Generally, these plants are grown as autumn crops because they favor cool, frost-free weather to develop the best flavor. In the South, cabbage is grown as an autumn and winter crop. Most catalogs list maturity periods as the date the transplants are set into the garden until they are ready to harvest.

Late-season cole crops are best started indoors or in cold frames and grown to transplant size; then set them into the garden, timing them to mature as cooler weather prevails. These vegetables are set in rows that are spaced 2½ to 3 feet (75 to 90cm) apart; plants are

Beautiful Cole Crops

Cabbages	Cauliflower	Broccoli
'Orange Bouquet'	'BurgundyQueen'	'Paragon'
'Promassa Baby'	'Chartreuse II'	'Romanesco'
'Savoy'	'Primavoy'	
'Red Royale'	'Roma Red'	
'Savoy King'	'Snow Mound'	
'Violet Queen'		

spaced 18 inches (45cm) apart. Top-dress generously with compost as the transplants are set. For more intensive planting, they can be planted in blocks with similar spacing. These spacing requirements should be respected, as cole crops are heavy feeders, demanding much in the way of nutrients and water during the growing season. They can be top-dressed again with compost or manure when the heads start to form. All cole crops benefit from a good layer of mulch.

During the growing season cole crops need to be watched for damage from cabbage butterfly larvae. These 1½-inch-long (3.5cm) green caterpillars will eat away at the leaves and destroy the plants if they are left unchecked. They are easily controlled with regular spraying of the organic spray BT.

Many types of cabbages are available from good seed catalogs. Early-season cabbages with shorter maturity periods are well suited to salads and slaws, and late-season cabbages are more suitable for long-term storage. Red cabbage is highly ornamental. Savoy cabbages,

with their beautiful crinkled leaves, are available in both early- and late-season types. They are preferred by many because of their attractive appearance and fine flavor, and make a superior addition to the kitchen garden.

Self-blanching types of cauliflower feature leaves that wrap around the head as it forms. If the cauliflower you are growing is not self-blanching, tie the leaves up around the head before it reaches the size of a small fist.

Cauliflower and broccoli are no longer limited to the traditional colors of white and green. New, more colorful varieties in lavender, purple, yellow, ivory, and lime green add a great deal to the kitchen garden. See the inset on this page for more colorful varieties of these vegetables.

CORN

Corn is a true favorite of North American gardeners. It is one of those vegetables best eaten just a few minutes out of the garden. Newer, super-sweet and sugar-enhanced varieties feature more tender kernels and a somewhat sweeter taste that will hold longer after the corn has been picked than normal types. These desirable features can be adversely affected by soil and growing conditions, however. Home gardeners who can pick and eat their corn within minutes may be better off growing a standard hybrid sweet corn. Whether you grow

TOP: Cabbages need plenty of room in which to mature. Here, fast-growing lettuce is situated between the young cabbage plants to make use of the space until the cabbages grow larger. BOTTOM: Sweet corn is among the most beloved of kitchen garden crops. These ears are full and the kernels are well formed.

A stunning pink-veined cabbage grows among salad greens and flowers.

standard sweet corn or one of the modern counterparts, make sure to choose a variety that is suited to your region.

Corn needs space in which to grow. If you are considering it for your garden, be sure to give it the space it needs. Rows should be 1 to 1½ feet (30 to 45cm) apart and you should grow a minimum of four rows side by side so that the wind may pollinate the plants. The best pollination is had by planting many long rows together. Therefore it is usually best to give corn a spot all its own.

Corn seed is sown in trenches 2 inches (5cm) deep in clay soils, deeper in sandy soils. Place the seeds 12 inches (60cm) apart in the trench. A good practice is to plant two seeds in each spot where you wish a plant to grow. If both seeds germinate, one can be culled when the plants are 4 to 6 inches (10 to 15cm) high. This ensures that you will have plants in each spot even if germination is not the best.

Corn feeds heavily on the soil and likes plenty of moisture. Extra compost or composted manure is always welcomed by this vegetable, and can be applied at any time up to when the tassels begin to form.

If you cannot wait for the late corn crop to come in, short-season varieties are available. The ears do not have the flavor or size of the later types, but to many enthusiasts it is well worth growing. As always, choose a variety that is well suited to your region.

CUCUMBERS, SQUASH, MELONS, AND PUMPKINS

Cucumbers and their relatives, or curcurbits, as they are called, have many things in common. All are vine crops, and most sprawl and spread their way through the garden unless tamed to a fence or trellis. Most summer squash and zucchini, however, are bushy vines and do not need to be trellised. They all feed

Crookneck varieties of summer squash are prolific, and several fruits may form at once. Picking them while they are young ensures that the crop will keep coming.

Spacing for Vine Crops

Crop	Planted in Hills	Trained to Fencing
Cucumbers	4–6 feet (1.2–1.8m)	4–6 feet (1.2–1.8m)
Squash	6–8 feet (1.8–2.4m)	8 feet (2.4m)
Melons	4–6 feet (1.2–1.8m)	4–6 feet (1.2–1.8m)

heavily on the soil, and in fact will dwindle if the soil is lacking in nutrients.

Most cucumber and summer squash varieties take 45 to 65 days to come to fruition. Winter squashes mature in 75 to 100 plus days depending on the type you grow. Pumpkins take 95 to 120 days to maturity, while melons, the most challenging of the lot, mature in 75 days or more, depending on variety.

All curcurbits are started in the same manner. In warmer regions they may be direct-seeded in the garden when the soil has warmed sufficiently. In northern areas it is best to start them early. Seeds may be sown in plastic pots or peat pots two to four weeks before the last expected frost, and the seedlings nurtured in a cold frame until they are ready to be transplanted into the garden. They are tender to cold, but respond to heat well, so they should not be planted in the garden until the soil has warmed. Many gardeners lay black plastic over the soil where they intend to plant these crops. Leaving the plastic in place for a week or two heats the soil, assuring that it is warm enough to sustain the seedlings. Remove the plastic when you are ready to plant your seeds or transplants, and replace it with a topdressing of composted manure and a layer of organic mulch.

During the growing season curcurbits need plenty of water; don't let the soil dry out. An extra topdressing of manure or compost is always most welcome.

Many folks plant their curcurbit crops in small "hills." These slightly raised mounds of

Mini Pumpkins

Cultivars for the Kitchen Garden

'Jack be Little'

'Sweetie Pie'

'Baby Boo'

'Spooktacular'

'Little Lantern'

soil keep excessive water away from the plant roots and away from the fruit. Fruits that lay on wet ground will rot quickly and are not likely to survive to maturity. Plant six to eight seeds in each hill, and when the seeds germinate cull them down to the three or four most viable seedlings (simply pluck out the seedlings you want to get rid of). Spacing for these hills and for regular rows of curcurbits vary; for traditional spacing requirements, consult the chart on page 52.

One way to save space when growing curcurbit crops is by trellising them so that they grow up instead of out. Cucumbers, melons, smaller winter squash vines, and mini pumpkins can be rotated with peas or pole beans on

permanent trellises in the garden. The vines will need to be trained to the trellis when they first begin to grow. Trellising also keeps the fruit off the ground and in good condition. You may experience problems with the weight of larger fruits when grown on trellises. The trellis or fencing must be sturdy enough to hold the weight of several fruits. Sometimes the fruits dangle precariously from the trellis as they mature. Ingenious gardeners solve this problem by swaddling the fruit with an old nylon stocking to help carry the weight. The stocking is tied to the trellis on both ends and helps support the weight of the fruit, but the fruit can still grow and mature in the flexible material.

You can also save space by choosing varieties that grow compactly. Bushy summer squash and zucchini take up little space, and one or two plants each can satisfy the most enthusiastic family appetite. Winter squash vines vary in size—butternut, buttercup, and acorn types sport much smaller vines than longer-term and more vigorous old-fashioned hubbard vines. Miniature pumpkins can be easily grown on trellises and make as nice a display in autumn as the larger fruited types. Old-timers grew their larger pumpkins in the cornfield to save space. Melons and cucumbers are easy to train to trellises if saving space is a priority.

LETTUCE AND SALAD GREENS

Gardeners all over the world enjoy preparing and eating salads fresh from the garden, and gone from their plates are greens that feature bland and colorless "iceberg" lettuces. You, too, can have an extraordinary salad garden within your kitchen garden.

Lettuces and salad greens are easy and rewarding to grow. Whether your taste runs to leaf, bibb, or head lettuce, a delightful variety awaits you. Along with lettuce, there are several other salad greens that you can grow to add

Nothing speaks more of autumn than a display of pumpkins. These 'Connecticut Field' types look stunning atop a well-constructed stone wall.

tang, flavor, and nutrition to your salads. Mustard greens, mache, arugula, cress, endive, and mesclun are salad greens that are easily added to garden plots.

Today's seed catalogs feature lettuces of every kind—lettuces with oak-leaf-shaped, red, crinkled, and deep green leaves abound. And these more sophisticated lettuces are packed with nutrition that iceberg lettuces cannot match.

Lettuces and salad greens are cool-season crops. For most gardeners they are crops of early spring to early summer and late summer to autumn. Lettuce is particularly sensitive to heat, and will bolt when hot weather persists. When it bolts, it grows upright, deteriorates, and goes to seed. For warmer climates cos lettuce is recommended because it stands up to heat much better.

Most leaf lettuce matures in 40 to 55 days, while head types can take as long as 90 days to mature. Succession planting, or making small plantings at weekly intervals, is recommended for continuous harvest.

Lettuce is planted in shallow drills, or trenches, at a depth of ¼ inch (0.6cm). To plan for lettuce with long maturity periods, sow seeds indoors early in the season, and then transplant them out into the garden. Lettuce likes cool temperatures, but is sensitive to frost, so care must be taken with spring seedlings.

Most lettuce and salad greens like a well-limed soil with a pH of 7. The soil should be high in nitrogen and have plenty of moisture. Topdressings of compost or composted manures and extra waterings are always appreciated.

The biggest enemy of salad greens and lettuce is slugs. Active at night, slugs crawl into the leaves and heads of lettuce—an unwelcome sight when you are about to make a salad. For tips on controlling slugs, see page 46.

Mustard greens add a tangy flavor to salads. Leaves can be harvested about 45 days

The wall bordering this garden doubles as a support for pole beans; salad greens grow in plots below them.

from planting in early spring or autumn, when they are just 4 inches (10cm) long. Mustard greens have a sharp peppery bite and can be cooked if desired.

Cress also adds a peppery bite to the salad bowl. Watercress can be grown at the edge of a stream or in waterlogged pots. Curly cress (grown in light shade) and broadleaf cress are good substitutes if you don't have a stream or pond. Curly and broadleaf cress are ready to harvest in less than 35 days, watercress in about 55 days. All are cool-season crops. Successive plantings and harvesting when the greens are young and tender are recommended.

Arugula, also known as rocket salad or roquette, is a peppery salad green that matures in just 45 days. Beloved in Europe, the oaklike leaves are ready to pick at 3 inches (7.5cm) long. Arugula requires little when it comes to

care. Successive plantings provide greens all spring and autumn.

Mache, or corn salad, takes 70 to 80 days to mature. In cold climates it can be sown in the autumn for spring harvest. This cool-season green has a rich taste that some people describe as nutty, and its flavor is welcome in salads or alone as a delicacy.

Mesclun is actually a mix of greens—lettuces, choi, kales, mustards, and endives. The exact mix depends on the palate it was designed to please. Mesclun is ready to harvest in 30 days or less; the leaves can simply be sheared with scissors. Designed as a "cut and come again" addition to the garden, the plants will rapidly regrow if they are watered and top-dressed with compost. Mesclun is tangy and flavorful alone or added to other salad greens.

Endive and escarole are autumn salad greens prized for their curly, crispy leaves. Both can be eaten in salads or sauteed as a side dish. Endive and escarole take 80 to 100 days to mature and are best grown as an autumn crop. In the northern areas, seeds sown in late June are ready for harvest in the autumn.

The leaves of endive and escarole can be left green or may be blanched. Green leaves are more bitter, but are also more nutritious. Blanched leaves turn white and lose their bitter flavor. Blanching must be done when the plant

OPPOSITE, TOP: This well-maintained vegetable plot makes use of a sunken brick edging to hold back the advancing lawn. The split rail fence is festooned with shrub roses that, come autumn, will hold heat in this garden, perhaps staving off frost a bit longer than could otherwise be expected. OPPOSITE, BOTTOM LEFT: Terracing is another way to use vertical space; these beds hold an array of lettuce, basils, and mustards. The tripods will support pole beans later in the growing season. OPPOSITE, BOTTOM RIGHT: Simple beauty can be found in every corner of the kitchen garden, as evidenced by the texture and color of these radicchio leaves.

is nearly mature and the inner leaves are totally dry. Tie up the outer leaves over the head of the plant with string. Leaves will blanch in about 10 days.

Radicchio, or red chicory, is another gourmet salad green. As with the other greens covered here, radicchio is a cool-weather crop. Radicchio matures in 60 to 75 days and can be grown as a spring or autumn crop. It is perhaps the most colorful of salad greens, sporting beet red leaves with white ribs. Like many of these greens, radicchio can be eaten in salad or sauteed as a side dish.

ONIONS AND LEEKS

Onions and leeks are staples in the kitchen garden. In most areas they can be grown successfully with a little advice, research, and experience. You can grow enough storage onions in one season to provide for your needs all winter long. Beautiful storage and sweet onions as well as leeks are within the reach of most gardeners.

Many people grow onions from sets because it is the easiest way. I think this is a mistake because onions from sets usually produce storage onions that are unremarkable except for their adaptability to a wide geographic area. If you desire sweet onions or something above the norm, you should be growing your own onions from seed.

Choosing the variety of onion to grow is most important, so study catalog descriptions carefully. Onions grow foliage in the cooler weather of spring and early summer, then set bulbs in the hotter weather. Onion plants are "day-length sensitive," which means that varieties differ in the length of day they require to

Harvested onions should be left on the ground to dry for a day or two, then set in a sheltered spot to dry thoroughly. Once completely dry, they should be cleaned and stored in a cool, frost-free place.

make a bulb. Those varieties that require longer daytime hours may not form bulbs in areas where the days are shorter in midsummer—such as areas in the South. Some catalogs will tell you the latitude to which each onion variety is adapted—a great advantage—so that you can choose one that will definitely bulb up in your garden.

Now that you have onions that will form bulbs, all you need to be concerned with is taste! Even though the famous 'Walla Walla' sweet onion appears to be a winner in upstate New York, in other areas the flavor may become too pungent due to the onion plant's response to soil or other conditions. In this regard, only the advice of another gardener who grows onions from seed in your area can replace a few years of experience.

A bed of onions is dressed up with a planting of white impatiens.

Bunching onions grown for scallions are much less complicated because the onions are picked in an immature state.

Leeks are related to onions, though they have a milder flavor, and are easy to grow from seed. Many gardeners blanch the shaft of the leek as it reaches maturity. The result is a delicate flavor unattainable by any onion.

Leeks and onions are easy to start from seed as long as it is fresh. Plant them indoors in pots ten to twelve weeks before they are to go into the garden. They should be hardened off in a cold frame earlier than other vegetables—approximately six weeks before the last expected frost. These plants appreciate cold weather as long as they are not in danger of freezing. Transplant the seedlings into the garden bed about the time of the last expected frost. Onions can be grown intensively as long as the soil is fertile. Space seedlings 5 to 6 inches apart (12.5 to 15cm). Double or triple rows of onions 12 inches (30cm) apart make good use of space in the garden. Keep seedlings well watered until they are established.

Leeks are grown in the same way as onions, but are not harvested until midautumn when they are mature. Seedlings should be set out about 12 inches (30cm) apart in double or triple rows 18 inches (45cm) apart. Leeks feed heavily on the soil over a very long season, so a topdressing of extra compost is always welcome. To blanch the stalks, many gardeners

plant them in a trench about 10 inches (25cm) below soil level, then gradually fill in the trench with compost as they begin to mature.

PEAS

If childhood memories conjure up unpleasant memories of pale canned peas, you owe it to yourself to try this wonderful vegetable as it was meant to be. Its flavor increases exponentially when picked and eaten fresh. "English" or garden peas, snap peas, and edible pod, or snow, peas are cool-season crops. All are grown in the same way. In northern areas they are

The succulent pods of these 'Green Arrow' peas are just starting to fill. Peas, above all other vegetables, should be eaten fresh from the garden.

grown as a spring crop, planted in March and picked in July; in the South and Southwest, they are grown as an autumn crop.

Peas need support from fencing or trellising in order to be productive. Because they enrich the soil with nitrogen, peas are often followed in succeeding years by crops that feed heavily on the soil. Fencing therefore needs to be mobile, or able to accommodate these other crops.

Other books, magazine articles, and seed packets will give you careful instructions on planting peas, but we have our own method. My husband has been admired and envied by many a gardener who has seen his ability to produce incredible crops of peas, and I have his permission to pass along the technique he uses. First, plant as early in the spring as you can. Dig a trench about 4 inches (10cm) deep using a hoe. Soak the seeds overnight in cool water, drain, and treat the seeds with legume inoculant. Do not place the seeds in the trench at 2-inch (5cm) intervals as is usually recommended, but instead spread handfuls of seeds thickly along the bottom. Putting the seed in a cardboard half-gallon milk container will allow you to pour the seeds into the trench. Cover the seeds and firm the soil over the top. The thickly sown plants will support each other as they grow. When the seedlings begin to break the soil, put up the fence supports if they are not already in place. Keep the peas watered, especially as they begin to blossom. They will also benefit from a good layer of mulch between the rows. Rows should be placed 2½ to 3 feet (75 to 90cm) apart, leaving enough room for you to move freely during the harvest.

By early summer you will be enjoying fresh peas at your table and freezing them for future use. The peas will not continue to bear, but will be done in by the hot weather of summer. Pea vines can be pulled out or turned under to enrich the soil. Follow them with a crop of cabbage, cauliflower, broccoli, beans, or another vegetable.

SWISS CHARD

Swiss chard is arguably the finest garden green that you can grow. It is both rich in nutrition and beautiful to look at. Swiss chard is a simple and easy crop to grow, producing a cut-and-come-again harvest all summer long. In the hottest climates, it may need to be replanted if it becomes affected by hot weather.

Swiss chard requires little care. Plant seeds in shallow drills 1 inch (2.5cm) apart. Germination of the seed is helped along if the seeds are soaked overnight in warm water. Swiss chard can be intensively planted in rows about 15 inches (38cm) apart. When the seedlings emerge, thin them to stand 8 inches (20cm) apart in the rows. A topdressing of compost or composted manure gives a boost to young plants.

Harvest the leaves by cutting them at the base of each plant with scissors. A topdressing of compost and a good watering will ensure that the plants regrow quickly for another harvest.

Several varieties of Swiss chard give color to the kitchen garden, and each has its own shade of crinkled leaves. Standard chard is a deep green color. Ruby, or rhubarb, chard has become very popular for the bright red leaves. A new variety, 'Joseph's Coat', has stalks in a range of colors—orange, red, white, and yellow—and is highly recommended as an ornamental plant for the kitchen garden.

ROOT CROPS—PARSNIPS, CARROTS, BEETS, RUTABAGAS, AND TURNIPS

Although all these root crops are different, they have many things in common. All like the soil

'Ruby Red' Swiss chard is certainly one of the most beautiful vegetables to grow, and is loaded with vitamins.

Beets offer a double harvest: the root is sweet and the greens are delectable when drizzled with a flavored vinegar.

This plot illustrates an undeniable fact of vegetable gardening; not all crops will mature at once. Instead, some crops come and go as the season passes, while longer-term crops persist through the year.

to be well drained yet moist, with good nutrient content. Potassium is particularly important in growing good root crops. Stones and other debris in the soil are resented, and can result in misshapen vegetables. Prepare the soil well and prepare it deeply, removing as many of the stones as possible from the area in which you intend to grow root crops.

Carrot seeds should be sown ¼ inch (0.6cm) deep in drills. Intensively planted drills can be located 10 to 12 inches (30cm) apart in good soils. Germination of carrot seeds can be unpredictable. For this reason, sow them—about six seeds per inch (2.5cm)—and cover with compost to help retain moisture evenly until the seedlings come up. When seedlings are 3 inches (7.5cm) tall, thin the carrot plants so they are about ¾ inch (2cm) from each other. When the young carrots get to finger size, they can be thinned again to be spaced about 2 inches (5cm) apart in the rows. Carrots can be planted in waves, allowing for successive harvests through the growing season.

Parsnips require a fair amount of work to get going, but need little care as the season progresses. Parsnip seeds are flat and lightweight, and if planted poorly will not germinate well. My husband uses the following procedure each year and gets excellent results. Soak the seeds overnight in cool water. Prepare the row, making sure that the soil surface is smooth, fine, and level. Water the row well, allowing the moisture to soak into the top layers of the soil. Place the seeds on the surface of the soil, spacing them evenly. Using your hands, sprinkle a fine layer of compost over the seeds, just barely covering half of each seed or so. Water again, gently, taking care that the seeds are not displaced by the water. Cover the length of the row with a wooden board—this will keep the soil moist.

Keep the soil moist in the row, lifting the board to water gently if necessary. Parsnip seeds are very sensitive and will not germinate if they dry out, even for a short period of time. After about two weeks begin to check for signs of germination. Leave the board in place until the parsnips begin to germinate. Remove it at the first sign of germination.

When seedlings are about 3 inches (7.5cm) high, thin them to stand about 8 to 12 inches (20 to 30cm) apart in rows, to allow for the ultimate width of the parsnips. Other than regular watering, parsnips need nothing until they are ready to harvest.

Because the flavor is vastly improved by cold weather, parsnips are traditionally left in the garden longer than any other vegetable. In northern areas they are harvested in early spring before they begin to grow again. In southern areas they can be harvested after several weeks of freezing weather has improved their flavor.

Beets can be grown in the same manner as other root crops, and also lend themselves to successive planting. Seed germination is enhanced by soaking the seeds overnight in warm water. Sow the seeds in drills ½ to ¾ inches (1 to 2cm) deep. When the seedlings reach 2 inches (5cm) in height, they should be thinned so that they are 3 inches (7.5cm) apart in the rows. This thinning must be done on a timely basis; if you wait too long the seedlings' growth will be retarded. Beets can be planted

intensively by spacing rows 12 to 15 inches (30 to 38cm) apart.

Beets are grown not only for the root, but also for the greens, which are delicious when cooked. Thinnings from beet plantings should never go to waste, and may be cooked as a side dish.

Many newer beet varieties add a bit of color to the table—some feature striped or yellow roots.

Rutabagas are perhaps the easiest root crop to grow. In northern areas, long-season (90 day) rutabagas are not planted until early summer, and mature about the time of the first frost. Rutabaga seeds are sown in drills ½ inch (1cm) deep. Thin the young plants when they are 3 or 4 inches (7.5 to 10cm) high. Due to their ultimate size, rutabagas should be thinned to 12 inches (30cm) apart. Rows spaced 15 to 18 inches (38 to 45cm) apart will give ample room for the rutabagas to mature fully.

Colorful Eggplant Cultivars

'Casper' (white)

'Rosita' (lavender)

'Italian Pink Bicolor' (purple-streaked white)

'Black Bell' (purple-black)

'Neon' (pink)

'Machiaw' (pink)

PEPPERS AND EGGPLANT

Peppers and eggplant are two of the most colorful vegetables you can include in the kitchen garden. Both are related to tomatoes and they are grown in the same fashion. For a reliable yield of either of these vegetables in northern areas, plants should be started early indoors. When you choose seed, make certain that the variety is meant to perform in your climate.

Peppers and eggplant should be started from seed at least eight weeks before they will be set in the garden. The transplants are particularly sensitive to cold, so do not rush them by placing them in cool garden soil. Doing so may set them back, and certainly will not help in any way. Transplants should be set in the garden when the weather has warmed reliably and the risk of frost has passed.

The flowers of peppers and eggplant, too, are sensitive to temperatures and this sensitivity can inhibit fruit set. Peppers in particular will not set fruit well if the temperature is too high or too low. Choosing varieties that are specifically geared to your area should ensure a bumper crop.

LEFT: A pink-skinned eggplant grows to maturity. OPPOSITE: Chili peppers and hot peppers come in diverse colors and an array of shapes and sizes— the ultimate good things in small packages.

Colorful Pepper Cultivars

Sweet	Hot
'Orobelle' (yellow)	'Numex' series (yellow)
'Islander' (purple)	'Valencia' (orange, purple, or red)
'Lipstick' (red)	'Pretty in Purple' (mix)
'Oriole' (orange)	'Habanero' (red)
'King' series (all colors, white)	'Golden' cayenne (gold)
'Klondike Bell' (gold)	'Chili Grande' (red)
'Super Sweet Banana' (white)	

Many people plant peppers and eggplant in rows. I have always planted them in blocks or patches, with each row spaced 1 foot (30cm) from the next. This layout is said to aid the pollination of the flowers, though this has never been proven. It does make good use of space, and my peppers have always thrived planted in this way.

Once the plants are set in the garden, they will enjoy a light fertilization with liquid kelp about once a month. Peppers are notorious for growing lush foliage but not setting fruit. This happens when the plants are given too much nitrogen, so make sure not to overfertilize.

Sweet peppers and hot peppers are both grown in the same manner.

Both peppers and eggplant offer a wide array of choices for the kitchen gardener these days, and fruits in all sizes, shapes, and colors can be found in most seed catalogs. Some are so ornamental that they can be easily blended into the flowers in the garden. For suggested varieties of peppers and eggplants see the insets opposite and above.

TOMATOES

Tomatoes are one of the most popular vegetables for the kitchen garden, and with good rea-son. No purchased tomato can match the flavor of a vine-ripened tomato from your garden.

There are an infinite number of varieties of tomatoes available from seed catalogs today. Some tomatoes are termed "determinate," which simply indicates that the vine ends, or terminates, in fruit. This tendency means that, for the most part, after the fruits have formed on each section of vine there will be no regen-eration of vine on which new fruit can form. Therefore, determinate tomato plants stop yielding after that fruit ripens.

Indeterminate tomatoes keep forming new vine, and therefore new fruit, all season

Tomato Cultivars of Merit

'Brandywine' (Amish heirloom—excellent flavor)

'Rutgers' (slicing tomato)

'Roma' (paste-type plum)

'Sweet Gold' (cherry tomato)

'Tigrette Cherry' (red and yellow–striped cherry tomato

'Moskvich' (Russian heirloom, early-maturing)

'German' (heirloom beefsteak)

long. Because of this tendency, indeterminate tomatoes yield heavy crops of fruit and produce all summer until frost. Indeterminate tomatoes also are bigger plants, needing more space in which to grow, and they are usually later-bearing than determinate tomato plants.

Once you choose between these two types, you will need to decide whether or not to stake your tomatoes. Many gardeners stake the indeterminate varieties because they sprawl and take up a lot of space. Staking generally reduces the overall yield because the vines will need to be pruned. This pruning adds significantly to the labor involved in growing tomatoes. If your soil is heavy and wet, you may want to stake your tomatoes just to keep them from rotting on the ground. Whether or not to stake tomatoes is a personal choice that most gardeners make after growing them both ways. I have never staked my tomatoes because I grow strictly for a heavy yield and do not like to add to my existing workload.

Tomato cultivars vary widely. There are big slicing types, cherry varieties, and paste tomatoes, each with a different size, shape, and/or use. I like to grow one or two cherry tomatoes simply because they ripen more quickly. You should choose varieties that suit your needs and taste. Many heirloom types that are packed with flavor are again available from seed catalogs. There are even types that are low in acid—these are not good for canning, but fine for folks who cannot tolerate acidic tomatoes. See the inset above for some suggested tomato varieties.

Tomatoes should be started indoors eight to ten weeks before they are to go in the ground. Transplants should be hardened off for at least two weeks in a cold frame. Set transplants in the ground 2 or 3 inches (5 or 7.5cm) deeper than the plant is growing in the container; this allows the stem to sprout roots, and the plant will develop a better root system.

Spacing of tomatoes in the garden depends on how they are grown and what type they are. Tomatoes that are not staked can be planted 2½ to 4 feet (.75 to 1.2m) apart in rows 3 feet (90cm) apart, depending on the type. If they are staked, spacing can be 18 to 30 inches (75cm) apart, depending on how they will be pruned.

OPPOSITE: Tomato sauce, whole canned tomatoes, chili tomatoes, pickled green tomatoes, and tomato preserves in every shade of red to green are a tomato connoisseur's delight! TOP: Tomatoes have undergone much experimentation through the years because they are true gardeners' favorites. The variety of sizes and colors of tomatoes available today is overwhelming. ABOVE: Cherry tomatoes are perfect for salads or snacking.

Chapter 4

kitchen garden herbs

The beauty, fragrance, and usefulness of herbs earn them a spot in every garden. A ready and healthful source of seasoning for your table, herbs are easy to care for, are generally pest-free, and take up very little garden space.

If you are a fan of herbal teas, you can easily grow enough herbs to provide a winter's supply of tea, and you can try your hand at blending a tea to suit your taste.

If it is potpourri that you adore, the herb section of your garden can yield a bountiful supply of leaves and petals to perfume your rooms throughout the year.

If you have never grown herbs, you have a treat in store. Studying herbs will introduce you to fascinating folklore and show you the myriad uses for herbs. And all the while, they contribute both ornamental value and practicality to the kitchen garden.

OPPOSITE: Blooms and fragrance for the table abound in this sunny summer border of herbs and flowers. Included are irises, sedum, Lamb's ears, gray santolina, and lavender. ABOVE: Ginger mint makes an attractive garnish and lends a spicy note to a refreshing drink on a summer afternoon.

Here you'll find the basics you need to know to grow healthy herb plants. Individual herbs have been highlighted, and I've focused on species and cultivars that are proven performers in a garden setting. You'll also find suggestions for planting a "garden within a garden." Tea gardens and potpourri gardens are a few examples of small herb gardens that might be integrated into your kitchen garden.

Herb gardening is a pleasurable experience, and is a hobby that will bring you rewards for many years to come.

CULTURE OF HERBS

Generally speaking, herbs are easier to grow than any other group of garden plants. They need less fussing, less water, less trimming, less spraying, and less soil preparation than other garden plants.

Many commonly grown herbs originate from the Mediterranean area. In their native habitat these plants struggle with low rainfall levels, wind, and poor soil. It is this struggle that encourages oil production in these herbs. The production of these essential oils sets many herbs apart from the rest of the plant world, and in your garden you want to try to re-create the conditions that enhance oil production.

Plants that fall into this category include thyme, rosemary, lavender, oregano and marjoram, sage, savory, dill, hyssop, horehound, lemon balm, burnet, and many other herbs that are not as widely grown. To grow these plants, it is best to not amend the soil too much. The soil should also drain very well, so that it dries out regularly, and should not be overly rich in nitrogen or nutrients. Herbs do respond to a periodic dose of rock phosphate, lime, or greensand. Because of their unusual preferences, you may want to leave the soil where these herbs are to be grown unamended except for those additions mentioned.

Herbs and flowers cut and hung in small bunches can be dried in a garden shed or garage out of the bleaching rays of the sun.

Even though many herbs enjoy these challenging conditions, there are some that prefer the regular garden conditions that you will have in vegetable or flower plots. Herbs that like a more nutrient-rich soil include parsley, basil, French tarragon, chives, garlic, lovage, angelica, borage, and sweet cicely. These herbs also prefer a more generous dose of water during the growing season than do herbs from more arid regions.

Herbs must have as much sunlight as you can give them. Although some will do well with just six hours of sun, most of your herbs will be much better off with no shade at all. There are a few exceptions to this rule, and the herbs that tolerate shade have been noted in the individual listings in this chapter.

Herbs to Dry and Hang

Bee balm (flowers)
Boneset (flowers)
Costmary (flowers)
Dill (flowers)
Echinacea (flowers)
Hyssop (flowers)
Lamb's ears (flower stalks)
Lavender (flowers)
Oregano (flowers)
Rue (seedheads)
Sage (stems)
Tansy (flowers)
Wormwood (flowers)
Yarrow (flowers)

HARVESTING AND STORING HERBS

Knowing when to harvest herbs is important. Many, like parsley and chives, can be harvested at any time. Others should be harvested when their essential oils are at their peak, which usually occurs just as the flowers are starting to open. Herbs that do not dry well can then be minced and frozen. Herbs that do dry well should be bundled in small bunches and hung in a warm dark place to dry. If bunches cannot be made, the herb can be dried flat on a clean screen.

Once the herb is very dry, strip the leaves from the stems. The leaves will store best and retain more flavor if they are left unbroken until you are ready to use them. Place them in an amber glass container. Label and date the container and leave it in a conspicuous spot for about two weeks. Check the container daily for any sign of condensation. If moisture forms, the herb is not thoroughly dry. Remove it from the container and continue the drying process. When you are sure the herb is completely dry, store the herbs in a cool dark location.

If you own a dehydrator, herbs can be dried easily in it. Keep the heat set no higher than 105 degrees to retain the precious essential oils.

HERBS FOR TEAS

If you are an herbal tea lover, consider planting a tea garden within your kitchen garden. Most tea herbs take up very little space and require little care. Prepare the soil as you would for other herbs.

When you begin to harvest for tea, experiment with your own garden's blend, trying different combinations of herbs until you find your favorite. If you enjoy black or green teas, try adding just a bit of your favorite tea herb to the brew to perk up the flavor. Experimenting is half the fun! You can buy empty tea bags from mail-order sources and give your own private blend as gifts to friends.

A POTPOURRI GARDEN

Because the herbs used in potpourris are often flowering herbs, a potpourri garden will be an

Spearmint is among the most popular herbs for teas.

Tea Herbs

Lemon Flavors

Lemon verbena

Lemon balm

Lemon thyme

Lemongrass

Mint Flavors

Spearmint

Applemint

Blue balsam tea mint

Orange or bergamot mint

Anise Flavors

Anise seed

Fennel

Anise hyssop

Fruity Flavors

Scented geraniums (fruit-scented selections)

Pineapple sage

Basic Flavors (Safe Medicinals)

Chamomile (relaxing)

Hyssop flowers (colds)

Catnip (sedative)

Bee balm (colds)

Angelica (sweet)

Ginger (spicy)

especially ornamental part of your kitchen garden. Cut flowers and leaves for potpourri in the morning after the dew has dried. Trim off the stems and remove the petals from the flowers. Spread the petals and leaves in a single layer and dry them in a cool dark spot. To make potpourri, simply mix together the dried petals and leaves and sprinkle them with a fixative—powdered orris root is often used. Place the potpourri in an airtight jar and store it in a

The flower petals and leaves of herbs make lovely natural potpourris for your home.

Herbs for Potpourris

Anise hyssop (flowers and leaves)

Anise (seeds)

Basil (flowers and leaves)

Bay (leaves)

Bee balm (flowers and leaves)

Borage (flowers)

Catnip (leaves and flowers)

Costmary (leaves)

Elderberry (flowers)

Hyssop (flowers)

Juniper (berries)

Lavender (flowers)

Lemon verbena (leaves)

Marjoram (flowers)

Mint (leaves and flowers)

Orris (root)

Rose (flowers)

Rosemary (leaves)

Sassafras (root)

Scented geranium (flowers and leaves)

Sweet woodruff (leaves)

Thyme (leaves)

ALPINE
STRAWBERR
'ALEXANDRIA'

Ever-bearing strawberries and miniature oranges grow amid an impressive collection of herbs in this imaginative tea garden.

cool, dark place until you are ready to set it out.

Experiment with different combinations of fragrant herbs and flowers til you find one (or several) that you like. Make sure to note the ingredients and proportions as you mix your potpourri so that you can re-create your successes and avoid duplicating your mistakes.

TWELVE ESSENTIAL HERBS FOR THE KITCHEN GARDEN

It is difficult to choose only a dozen representatives from the expansive list of herbs that can be grown in the kitchen garden. I have, however, confined the list to the herbs that are of the most interest and benefit to the kitchen gardener—which of course means that for the most part I have listed herbs for cooking. Some of the herbs listed have dual purposes, which have been noted.

BASIL (*OCIMUM BASILICUM*)

Basil is an important herb that is grown primarily as an annual in the garden. Basil is native to areas of India, Asia, and Africa.

All basil varieties like rich, moist, slightly acid soil and lots of sun. Basil plants are particularly sensitive to cold, and plants will deteriorate in temperatures lower than 40 degrees. Therefore, it is a good practice to avoid planting basil outdoors until warm weather has arrived and the soil is warm. Young plants are particularly sensitive.

Many varieties of basil are available from seed. The differences in these varieties are either in aroma and flavor or in the leaf type. Ornamental types with crinkled or red leaves make an attractive addition to any garden.

Basil is one of the most widely used culinary herbs. The flavor it imparts to meats, sauces, and tomato dishes is legendary. Basil

can also be drunk as a tea to calm an upset stomach or anxiety. Basil tea also makes a good hair rinse for brunettes, restoring luster to the hair. The aromatic leaves of holy basil, lemon basil, and anise basil lend themselves particularly well to potpourris.

Basil transplants can be purchased early in the spring from garden centers, or they are easily grown under lights. Seed should be started six to eight weeks in advance of the date the

---

Basil Varieties

All are cultivars of *Ocimum basilicum*, unless otherwise noted.

'Large Sweet' (green; large plant; good producer)

'Anise' (green with purple cast; aniselike aroma and flavor)

'Cinnamon' (green; cinnamon aroma and flavor)

'Green Ruffles' (green with crinkled foliage; flavor similar to 'Large Sweet')

'Purple Ruffles' (red; flavor similar to 'Large Sweet'

'Minimum' (dwarf bush basil; good flavor; excellent for containers)

'Thai Basil' (green leaves, purple stems; wonderful exotic flavor)

'Mexican Basil' (green; sweet spicy flavor and aroma)

'Genovese' (green; selected from Italian stock; very flavorful)

'Opal' (red, smooth leaves; ornamental; good flavor)

'Spicy Globe' (green; mounding dwarf to 6" (15cm); excellent spicy flavor)

Ocimum sanctum (green; not culinary; best for potpourri; sweet fragrance)

O. americanum 'Lemon Basil' (green; delicate plant; lemony flavor)

---

plants will go in the garden. Starting your own basil plants is advantageous because it will allow you to grow varieties that garden centers do not stock.

Basil is one of the more difficult herbs to dry, because it tends to lose most of its flavor. The best method of storage is freezing. For the best flavor, pick basil just as the flowers are beginning to open. Rinse the stems to remove dust and debris. Strip the leaves off the stem and place them in a blender with just enough water to help liquify the herb. Blend until a smooth paste forms. Spoon the paste into cupcake baking cups, filling them with the approximate amount that you would use in cooking. Freeze the basil until solid. The baking cups can be stacked and stored in the freezer in labeled plastic bags.

ROSEMARY *(ROSMARINUS OFFICINALIS)*—HARDY TO ZONE 8

Rosemary is an important culinary herb from the arid region of the Mediterranean. In warmer climates it can be grown as a perennial, but in northern areas it will need to be planted every year. Rosemary is tolerant of dry, poor soils and should be grown in full sun.

There are several types of rosemary sold, most of which exhibit different habits or flower colors. Pine-scented rosemary has a piney, pungent fragrance and flavor, while 'Tuscan Blue' bears deep-colored flowers. Trailing rosemary is a prostrate form.

Purchase rosemary transplants to put in the garden when danger of frost has passed. If you start rosemary from seed, start seeds at least twelve to sixteen weeks before the plants are to go in the garden. Rosemary is a very slow-growing plant, especially in the seedling stage.

Rosemary is used in many types of dishes, and particularly on chicken, fish, and roasted red meats. It is also favored for sauces and salad dressings. In centuries past, rosemary was prescribed for stomach ills and as tonic. Rosemary tea also makes a wonderful hair rinse for brunettes.

OPPOSITE: The deep green leaves of sweet basil lend their flavor and aroma to many dishes and are also an ingredient in potpourris. Basil varieties differ and most are highly ornamental in the garden. BELOW, LEFT: A closeup of rosemary shows the arrangement of the fine needlelike leaves. BELOW, RIGHT: Flat-leaf, or Italian, parsley is unsurpassed as a garnish, flavoring, or salad green.

Rosemary can be harvested at any time, as long as the plant is of a substantial size. Dry rosemary for storage as you would other herbs, following the instructions on page 66.

PARSLEY *(PETROSELINUM CRISPUM)*

Parsley prefers full sun and good garden soil that is fairly rich in nutrients. Although it is a biennial, it is grown as an annual. Parsley planted the first year will yield a good harvest; the following year it can be harvested very early in the season. If left in the ground, it will send up a flower stalk and at this point is no longer good to harvest. It is far better to remove the plants after the first growing season and replace them early in the spring.

There are three types of parsley commonly sold. Flat-leaf Italian parsley is a large plant about 15 inches (38cm) tall and yields a fine harvest. Some say this parsley has the best flavor. Two dwarf types of parsley are available—one is called 'Flat Leaf' and the other is called 'Triple Curled'. 'Triple Curled' parsley is favored as an ornamental garnish for the dinner table. All varieties have wonderful flavor.

Parsley transplants can be purchased or you may start your own plants from seed. It is best to sow the seeds after placing them in the freezer for three weeks. This treatment will ensure quicker germination once the seeds are planted. Start seeds indoors in January or February and set them out after threat of frost has passed.

Parsley is most often used in salads, creamed dishes, and with meats of all kinds. It is high in Vitamin C, vitamins A and B, calcium, and iron.

Parsley can be harvested at any time during the growing season, but is difficult to dry in the traditional way. It can be frozen more easily. Mince it finely and place it in freezer bags for storage.

CHIVES *(ALLIUM SCHOENOPRASUM)*— HARDY TO ZONE 3

Chives are one of the most easily grown herbs. They are perennial and require regular to rich garden soil and full sun. Their cheery pink flowers are edible and can be used in spring salads. Related to onions, they in fact grow from small bulbs. Chives grow in clumps, which quickly expand and can be divided.

Chives may be purchased from a garden center, but are very easily started from seed. Seedlings require one growing season before they should be harvested. Seeds should be planted indoors six to eight weeks before the last expected frost.

Garlic chives *(Allium tuberosum)* are also useful in the garden. They sport white flowers in autumn and have a distinct garlic flavor. Take care not to allow the seeds to scatter in the garden, as garlic chives can be difficult to eradicate.

Chives and garlic chives are used mainly for cooking in creamed dishes, salads, potato dishes, and with meat or vegetables of any kind.

Chives may be harvested at any time during the growing season by simply snipping off the leaves you need. Chives are very difficult to dry. To prepare them for storage, rinse the leaves, mince them finely, place them in freezer bags, label, and freeze.

FRENCH TARRAGON *(ARTEMISIA DRACUNCULUS)*—HARDY TO ZONE 4

Tarragon is an elusive herb. The plant itself is less than unassuming, difficult to find, and tricky to keep going in the garden. Even so, good-quality tarragon is hard to find in the markets, and growing your own can be very satisfying.

Tarragon needs fairly rich soil in partial shade, and is never a vigorous grower due to a

rather spindly root system. To keep tarragon healthy year after year, the roots must be dug and divided. Keep only the most robust parts of the plant to reestablish the bed. This task should be done as early in the spring as you can manage.

Tarragon should never be started from seed. Seed sources are quite unreliable, and flavor and aroma vary widely from plant to plant. To assure the best quality, buy plants from a reliable mail-order source or buy aromatic plants from a good garden center. Beware that there is a plant called Russian tarragon that is commonly sold as simply "tarragon," and is passed off as the real thing. If it has no aroma, don't buy it!

Tarragon is most commonly used in chicken, fish, meats, and vegetable dishes, as well as creamed dishes and sauces. To best preserve the flavor of tarragon, make tarragon vinegar or mince it finely and store in freezer bags or containers. Tarragon may be harvested any time during the growing season.

THYME *(THYMUS VULGARIS* AND OTHER SPECIES)—*T. VULGARIS* HARDY TO ZONE 5, MOST SPECIES HARDY TO ZONE 4

Thyme is one of the easiest herbs to grow and offers many choices in growth habit and flavor. It prefers a dry, poor soil in full sun, and in most cases is a reliably hardy perennial.

Common garden thyme *(Thymus vulgaris)* is actually a small shrublike plant, and because it is evergreen it can struggle in extreme northern climates during a bad winter. The lower-

OPPOSITE, LEFT: Bumblebees show a definite preference for chive blossoms. Bees of all kinds are invaluable pollinators in gardens throughout the world. OPPOSITE, RIGHT: Hyssop, tarragon, and dill—all culinary favorites—are easily cultivated in the kitchen garden. ABOVE: Because chives are both attractive and useful, they make an excellent edging for beds in the kitchen garden.

> ## Good Culinary Varieties of Thyme
>
> *Thymus vulgaris* (English garden thyme)
>
> *Thymus vulgaris* 'Narrow Leaf French'
>
> *Thymus* × *citriodorous* (lemon thyme)
>
> *Thymus herba barona* (caraway thyme)

growing thymes are also evergreen, but stand a much better chance of survival at ground level. When choosing a thyme to grow, you will be confronted not only with differences in habit but with differences in flavor. Lemon thyme is one of the most popular thymes. Other thymes recommended for their culinary value are listed under this heading.

Thyme is a very slow-growing plant and is a bit challenging to grow from seed. You will get better results by choosing a fragrant plant from a garden center or ordering from a reliable mail-order nursery.

All types of meat, poultry, stews, vegetables, and sauces are enhanced by the addition of thyme. This herb can be harvested at any point in the season, but flavor will be highest when the flowers are just beginning to open. Thyme can be dried in the traditional way detailed on page 66.

BRONZE FENNEL *(FOENICULUM VULGARE NIGRA)*—HARDY TO ZONE 4

The fernlike red foliage of bronze fennel is a stunning sight to behold in the garden. Bronze fennel is a perennial herb that grows tall and narrow, reaching a height of 4 to 5 feet (1.2 to 1.5m). This copper-foliage version of the traditional green fennel appears to be just slightly hardier than green fennel in northern gardens. In more moderate climates green fennel will be a reliable perennial. The two plants looks wonderful when they are grown side by side.

Fennel appreciates a rich, slightly moist soil in full sun. It is easily started from seed, but quicker results are to be had if plants are purchased from a garden center. If you do start fennel from seed, start it outdoors in mid-spring or indoors in small deep pots that will not confine the long tap root that is characteristic of this plant.

Fennel is noted for the aniselike flavor it imparts in cooking. The seeds are commonly used in teas, beverages, and baked goods, and have been used for centuries to flavor certain liqueurs. The bulb is used in sauces and stews. Fresh leaves are both beautiful and refreshing in salads, adding an unexpected flavor, and are also excellent with fish. Used fennel leaves fresh, as they do not store well. Fennel seed-heads can be collected and dried. Once dry, the seeds can be stripped off and stored in glass jars all winter long.

LAVENDER (*LAVENDULA ANGUSTIFOLIA*)—HARDY TO ZONE 5

Lavender, although not a culinary herb, is intensely popular because of the wonderful fragrance emitted by the entire plant. A woody perennial, it prefers a very well drained, slightly alkaline soil. A topdressing of lime each autumn and a topdressing of rock phosphate every three or four years will keep your lavender plants very happy. If your soil is soggy or wet, you will have difficulty growing this choice flowering herb.

OPPOSITE, TOP: Several varieties of thyme planted in a large terra-cotta pot are a decorative and practical accent for a rustic twig bench. OPPOSITE, BOTTOM: For those who inspect closely, thyme shows off its obvious charms in both foliage and flower. RIGHT: The reddish foliage of bronze fennel makes an excellent foil for any garden plant.

'Hidcote' lavender lines the brick path in this charming potager.

Because lavender is a woody plant, it has special pruning requirements. Prune plants right after flowers are harvested in the summer. Using pruners with a sharp blade, cut off any remaining flower stalks and about 3 inches (7.5cm) of foliage. If you do not prune the plants regularly, they will become leggy and spindly, and will only put out weak growth and few flowers. If by chance you have allowed your lavender plants to get into this state, prune them more severely until they are once again well shaped. Should you miss the chance to prune your lavender in midsummer, skip pruning them until the following spring.

There are many types of lavender native to different areas of the world. When purchasing lavender at a garden center, be certain that the plant is labeled with the botanical name and that the variety you choose is hardy in your area. Because lavender is a very slow-growing plant, you'll have the best results if you buy established plants.

Lavender is legendary for use in perfumes, potpourris, and cosmetics of every description. For the home gardener, harvesting the flowers for use is a simple matter. As soon as the flowers open, cut the flower stalk. Bundle several stalks together and fasten the ends with a rubber band. Hang these bunches upside down to dry. The flowers may be stripped from the stems and used in floral water, sachets, linen bags, or potpourri. For the best storage of the flowers, package them in tightly sealed plastic bags and use them within a year.

SAGE *(SALVIA OFFICINALIS)*—HARDY TO ZONE 4

Sage is one of the easiest herbs to grow, requiring only well-drained, average soil in full sun. Sage is a woody perennial and needs regular pruning to keep it in prime condition. After flowering in early spring, cut back all branches

about 6 inches (15cm). This will keep full, lush foliage coming year after year. Even with diligent pruning, sage will need to be replaced every seven or eight years.

There are several varieties of garden sage available, all of which are beautiful and useful in the kitchen garden. Variegated forms with gold- or white-edged leaves are quite popular and hardy. Another variegated selection, sometimes called tricolor sage, has white-and-pink-edged leaves, but is not hardy in more northern climates. Dwarf sage is sometimes available, as is a type known as 'Holt's Mammoth', which has extra-large leaves and is generally used for commercial production. Purple sage has beautiful burgundy-colored foliage and is highly ornamental in any garden setting.

OPPOSITE: 'Munstead' is a relatively compact lavender cultivar, and reaches only about 12 inches (30cm) in height. BELOW: The wonderfully marked leaves of golden variegated sage add color and fragrance to the herb border.

If you are inclined to start plants from seed, sage is an easy one to try. The seedlings grow to maturity more quickly than most other herbs and are not fussy in their requirements. To obtain variegated, purple, or dwarf sage, however, you must purchase vegetatively propagated plants either through the mail or at a garden center.

Known mainly for its culinary use in stuffings and meats, sage is also good with potatoes and cabbage. Sage tea makes a fine hair rinse for brunettes, and through the centuries sage has also been used in dyes and as an ingredient in many cosmetics.

Sage may be harvested any time during the growing season. Harvest and dry sage in the traditional way as detailed on page 66.

GREEK OREGANO (ORIGANUM HERA-CLEOTICUM)—HARDY TO ZONE 5

Greek oregano is an easy plant to grow, requiring well-drained, slightly acid soil and full sun. Give oregano some room to expand, as the somewhat creeping rootstock will enlarge your bed of this fragrant herb. There are several types of oregano commonly sold. Be wary of buying *Origanum vulgare,* or common oregano. This sometimes invasive plant has very little fragrance and flavor to recommend it, but is commonly sold as a culinary herb. Golden creeping oregano is attractive in the garden, and is acceptable as a culinary herb. In the interest of flavor it is best to purchase plants from a reliable mail-order nursery or garden center. Be sure that the plants you buy

OPPOSITE: The soft, elegant foliage of common sage overreaches its bounds, billowing onto the slate garden path. LEFT: Clay urns add architectural interest to this mixed plot of vegetables, herbs, and flowers.

While lacking some of the exuberance of a colorful flower bed, the herb garden offers a subtle charm all its own.

are labeled correctly and that they have a noticeable aroma.

Oregano is known for its place in Italian dishes, but is used heartily in many parts of the world. Meats, vegetables, and other herbs are enhanced by the addition of oregano. Harvest, dry, and store oregano in the traditional way detailed on page 66.

SUMMER SAVORY
(SATUREJA HORTENSIS)

Summer savory is too little known, but easily grown. It is not fussy, and likes average, well-drained garden soil. Summer savory is an annual herb, so replanting each year is necessary. Make sure to purchase fresh seeds each spring.

Savory is best if planted directly in the garden in shallow drills. Plant the seeds fairly thickly, as the plants themselves tend to be spindly and weak. It may be necessary to brace them with short fencing as they grow to maturity to keep them from being flattened by a heavy rain or wind. Summer savory is used primarily for cooking—potatoes, meats, fish, and most vegetables benefit from the addition of summer savory. In centuries past, summer savory was also used as a medicinal herb.

Summer savory can be harvested through the summer, but when the plants begin to flower the whole plant should be cut for harvest. Dry and store summer savory in the traditional way detailed on page 66.

Beautifully organized but informal plots offer herbs for culinary and household use, vegetables for the table, and flowers for cutting and garden ornament.

RIGHT: The gray foliage of curry plant and the red blooms of painted daisies share space with resplendent chive blossoms in this early-summer herb bed.
OPPOSITE: Herbal oils and vinegars put up in beautiful bottles make fabulous gifts.

Savory Wine Vinegar

This simple recipe can be adapted for any flavor of herb vinegar you choose. What better way to spend a summer afternoon than making an assortment of these tasty vinegars to give as gifts or to enjoy all winter?

A general formula is to use about 18 inches (45cm) of stem for each 2 cups (500ml) of vinegar you make. Stems can be cut into smaller pieces.

You will need:
Several summer savory stems, just begin-
     ning to flower
1 quart (1L) of red or white wine vinegar
Assorted attractive bottles with screw-on
     lids or corks

Wash the glass bottles thoroughly and sterilize them by dipping them in boiling water. Place several pieces of stem in each jar (about 9 inches [23cm] of stem for every cup [250ml] of vinegar the jar will hold). Heat the vinegar to just below the boiling point in a glass, enamel, or stainless steel pan. Fill each jar with vinegar while the vinegar is very hot. Cover and allow to cool. The vinegar will be ready to use in about two weeks.

A comfortable bench with a commanding view of the garden offers a quiet spot from which to enjoy the results of a day of garden chores.

reliable flowers

Flowers, whether they are perennial or annual, add several dimensions to the kitchen garden, including vibrant color, lush form, and enchanting fragrance. And while some vegetable gardeners scorn the "impractical" and ornamental nature of flowers, those who have enjoyed fresh cut flowers through the seasons and everlastings all year round make sure to include an array of inviting blooms. Attracting bees, butterflies, and birds to the landscape may also be reason enough to include certain flowers in the overall plan.

Annuals as well as perennials can be grown in the kitchen garden, although the approach for each is different. Annuals generally need richer soil than perennials, and are usually more vibrant in color. Garden space is also managed differently; while perennials remain in one spot, annuals can be planted in different places from year to year. Perennials last year after year in the landscape, and their flowers have more subtle charm than do annuals.

Peonies are one of the most beloved flowers of all time. Today's gardeners are fortunate to be able to choose from single-flowered varieties or double-flowered types like the peony pictured here.

ABOVE: This pretty cottage garden is at its peak in early to midsummer. Note the scarlet runner beans grown on a pole, the gray foliage of wormwood in bloom, and the drooping white flowers of nicotiana at left. OPPOSITE: Whether you are entering the garden or leaving it, this singular garden gate and a mix of flowering perennials create a lasting impression of summer at its finest.

Each perennial has a personality of its own and maintenance is more seasonal in nature. Most offer a bloom period of three to six weeks, so if you use them you will want to plan a succession of color for the garden beds. Of course, annuals and perennials can be mixed together tastefully. The flowers you choose for your landscape will reflect the cultural conditions as well as your personal taste. Room can be made for both perennials and annuals, or you may prefer one over the other. In any case, flowers in the landscape will reward you each time you glance at your kitchen garden.

In this chapter you will find many ideas for working flowers into your overall kitchen garden plan. General cultural information for annual and perennial flowers is also included here, and there are profiles for a few of the most outstanding flowers in each category. Although it is extremely difficult to choose the best of the many varieties available, the profiled flowers are proven performers. Because it isn't possible to discuss every flower available, you'll find several charts to consult when you are choosing plants for a particular situation; these suggest different flowers to consider. I

have deliberately emphasized old-fashioned and little-used flowers of particular merit.

ANNUAL FLOWERS FOR THE KITCHEN GARDEN

Annual flowers are flowers that grow to maturity, bloom, and die all in the space of one growing season. Because you want them to be in flower for as much of the growing season as possible, annual flowers should be started indoors early or purchased from a greenhouse grower. If annuals are to perform well, the growing conditions in which you place them must be first-rate, providing all they need to grow—and quickly.

To ensure that you get top performance from the annuals you choose, follow the cultural guidelines and tips provided below.

GENERAL TIPS

If you are starting your own plants from seed, get an early start. Purchase seeds from a reliable source. Seeds offered at bargain prices are rarely a good buy.

Most annual seeds need to be started two to three months before they are to be set into the garden. Getting an early start means that your transplants will come into bloom on schedule. Take some time to study what plants do well in your area by talking to other gardeners or through observation. Learn the conditions that are preferred by the plants you plan to grow. Do your best to accommodate them; if you cannot, perhaps there is a better choice for your garden.

SOIL

Most annual flowers need a fairly rich soil in order to thrive and grow quickly, and especially to come into bloom on schedule. If you have prepared the soil according to the information in the basics section of this book (see Chapter 1), your annuals should thrive.

WATER

Most annuals appreciate 1 inch (2.5cm) of water a week during the growing season. When you water, water deeply and thoroughly. If you are growing drought-tolerant plants, weekly watering is not necessary.

PLANTING TRANSPLANTS IN THE GARDEN

When the time comes to plant your annual flowers, they will benefit from an additional boost of water and nutrients. Using a trowel, dig a hole in which the transplant will go. Fill the hole with "fertilizer water" mixed to the specifications of the manufacturer. Liquid kelp works well for this process. Let the hole drain, then place the transplant in the hole and back-fill with soil. Make sure that the soil around the transplant is firm, and give the plant another drink of fertilizer water. Taking a little extra time to do this will get the plants off to a great start.

PLANTING STRATEGIES

While the style of your garden is largely a matter of personal taste, there are some tried and true gardening practices. Plants look better when planted in groups. Clumps of four to six plants of the same species make a strong statement in the garden.

Planting flowers in rows is not effective or visually pleasing unless, for example, a bed of all one type of plant is being edged with another of contrasting color or foliage.

Geometric patterns work well only if your plants are all vigorous. Replacement plants are good to have on hand should some fail to thrive during the growing season. To make planting these more complicated beds easier, consult the garden plans in Chapter 2.

Use foliage plants to your advantage. Sharp placement of plants with contrasting foliage can be just as beautiful as any flower bed, and the foliage will be there to enjoy all season long.

ANNUAL FLOWER PROFILES

COSMOS (*COSMOS* SPP.)

This simple daisy-shaped flower has been a garden favorite for many years. Cosmos are very colorful and come in nearly every shade and hue. Taller cosmos are grown in the back

Cosmos are easily grown and are available in many flower colors and several heights, making them quite adaptable in borders.

of the bed, and can top 4 feet (1.2m) in height. Newer, shorter types are becoming increasingly available and are quite popular.

The ferny foliage of cosmos is also attractive in the garden. Cosmos make good cut flowers, and thrive even in poorer soils. Some gardeners claim that they thrive on neglect, but they do require full sun. Cosmos are best started directly in the garden from seed.

IMPATIENS (*IMPATIENS* SPP.)

The versatile impatiens earns a place of honor among annuals. Even when planted in deep shade, the incredible volume of bloom derived from these plants has catapulted them to the top of every gardener's "must have" list. Impatiens are available in every color you can think of, including apricot and flaming orange. These vibrant colors go a long way toward brightening even the shadiest corner of the garden. Impatiens are adaptable to containers, hanging baskets, and window boxes, where it is somewhat easier to give them the nutrients and water they thrive on.

Impatiens can be raised from seed to ensure that you get the color you desire. To get the best results, start impatiens twelve weeks before the last expected frost. The seeds can be a bit tricky to start, but this is easily overcome. Prepare the packs in which the seeds are to be

New Guinea impatiens, with their bright flowers and ornamental foliage, brighten a shady corner of the garden.

A riot of color bursts from this annual bed featuring petunias, violas, marigolds, salvia, and celosia.

Annuals Grown for Their Scent

Monarda citriodora

Dianthus

Stocks

Sweet William

Four o'clocks

Heliotrope

Mignonette

Nicotiana

Phlox drummondi

'Lemon Gem' marigold

sown. Firm the soil and plant the seeds on the surface, but do not cover the seeds. Place a small piece of glass or rigid plastic over the seed flats and put them in a sunny window or, preferably, directly under a light. When the majority of seeds begin to germinate, you can remove the glass. Impatiens seedlings grow slowly. When they start to crowd the cells in which they are growing, transplant each seedling into a small pot of its own.

SALVIA (*SALVIA* SPP.)

Salvias are a diverse group of plants that offer a great deal of color for areas of the garden ranging from full sun to moderate shade. Annual salvia flowers are most often red or blue, but many newer varieties come in shades of pink, coral, and white.

The red flowers are a particular favorite of hummingbirds and butterflies, and are spectacular when planted in masses. Salvias are easily grown from seed to bloom in early summer. They are remarkably tolerant of hot, dry conditions. In the South some "annual" salvias grow as perennials.

Salvia farinacea is an annual salvia commonly grown for its flowers because they dry exceptionally well. It comes in white, and blue,

and in a new bicolored blue and white flower called 'Strata'.

SNAPDRAGONS (*ANTIRRHINUM* SPP.)

Snapdragons are not only old-fashioned flowers, they are great performers that bloom nearly all summer long, come in all colors, and are quite adaptable. Though they are grown as an

TOP: Snapdragons are an old standby for borders. Today they are available in standard colors as shown, as well as in more pastel shades. Grown as an annual in many areas, snapdragons reseed well and will live through the winter in many locations. BOTTOM: Salvia is popular for its long bloom time and variety of colors. OPPOSITE: This brilliantly colorful mixed flower bed includes dianthus, an annual often grown for its scent.

ABOVE, LEFT AND RIGHT: Sweet Williams combine fragrance with old-fashioned charm. There are many cultivars and a range of colors to choose from. OPPOSITE: Annuals and perennials are close neighbors in this sunlit flower border. When planting a border, it's advisable to place tall-growing flowers at the back, medium-height plants in the middle, and low-growing specimens in the foreground, so that all can be seen and enjoyed.

annual in northern areas, they sometimes return for a year or two, especially if you live in a milder climate.

I can remember my grandmother staking her "snaps" as she called them, to keep them from flopping over in the wind or rain. New shorter varieties make staking a thing of the past. Snapdragons bloom quite quickly when started from seed. They make good cut flowers and attract pollinating insects to the garden.

SWEET WILLIAM (*DIANTHUS BARBATUS*)

Sweet William is actually a biennial that is usually grown as an annual. If it comes back to your garden for a second year, you won't complain!

This flower is related to carnations and smells just as sweet. If you look closely at the flat clusters of flowers, you will see that the individual flowers look like miniature versions of carnations. Sweet William flowers are often

bicolored, and can range from delicate shades of pink or white to the deep magenta color for which they are beloved. Sweet William makes a wonderful cut flower.

If sown early enough, many varieties will bloom the first year from seed, and they are easily started indoors.

PLANTING AN ANNUAL BORDER

The simplicity of an annual border can fool you. If you just start placing plants with no forethought, you are bound to make mistakes.

There is a reasonable way to proceed to avoid some common pitfalls. First, make a list of the annuals you have designated for the area, and note approximately how many of each you have. Also list their height and approximate spread.

Prepare the garden soil and rake it smooth. Now you must begin to plan where groupings of plants will go. Use a fine dusting of lime to outline the outer edge of the first area. Do not work with straight lines and angles—curved edges look much nicer. Continue to define the different areas of the bed with lime. If you change your mind or make a mistake, simply brush it away and start over. Keep in mind the height and rough placement of annuals as you designate each area. As your plan solidifies, note the plants that will be placed in each location, putting taller plants in the rear and shorter plants to the front, and mixing foliage and flower color throughout the bed. Soon, you will be able to do much of this in your head.

PLANNING AN EVERLASTING GARDEN

If you are fond of everlastings, incorporate them into your kitchen garden plan. Using just a little space, you can grow an assortment of everlastings to dry and hang in your home or to use in dried arrangements.

To ensure that you get the flower color you want, grow your own transplants from seed. By adding one or two perennials such as baby's breath to the bed, you will have all you need to make wreaths and arrangements for the house.

Below are tried and true everlastings to grow in your garden. You should always buy dried flowers in separate colors—not color mixes—to get the most sought-after colors. Listed with each type of flower are the color selections that are most recommended.

Annual statice (*Limonium sinuatum*)—Sunset Shades, Iceberg, Rose, Deep Blue, Light Blue, Apricot, Roselight, Sirima hybrids

Dwarf winged everlasting (*Ammobium* 'Bikini')

Globe amaranth (*Gomphrena globosa* and

G. hoageana)—Lavender Lady, Rose, Pink, White, Strawberry Fields, Orange Globe

Hare's tail grass *(Lagarus ovatus)*

Immortelle *(Acrolinum)*

Love-in-a-mist (*Nigella damascena*)

Traditional straw flower *(Helichrysum bracteum* 'Monstrosum' and 'Bikini')—Pastel Shades, Rose, Silvery Rose, White

PLANNING A MOONLIGHT GARDEN

In Victorian days, moonlight gardens were very popular additions to the kitchen garden or estate. A moonlight garden usually consists of

Annuals for Constant Summer Bloom

Alyssum

Ageratum

Geraniums

Marigolds

Nasturtiums

Nicotiana

Petunias

Snapdragons

Impatiens

OPPOSITE: Edible flowers, including colorful yellow and red nasturtiums, make elegant garnishes for the table. ABOVE: A row of stones lends a rock garden aura to this planting. Colorful snapdragons will keep the border blooming all summer long.

Plants for the Moonlight Garden

Alyssum

Bishop's weed

Creeping baby's breath

Dame's rocket

Dusty miller

Evening primrose

Feverfew

Flowering tobacco

Formosa lily

Four o'clock

'Grey Lady' lavender

'Icicle' speedwell

Lamb's ears

Madonna lily

Moonflower

'Mount Fujiyama' summer phlox

Perennial baby's breath

Rose campion

Santolina

'Silver Mound' artemisia

Snow-in-summer

Spider flower

Sweet alyssum

White-flowered alpine pinks

White-flowered foxglove

White-flowered love-in-a-mist

'White Nancy' lamium

In a moonlight garden, flowers and foliage in white and silver are interplanted to create a soft glow in the waning light. Lamb's ears, 'Alba' rose campion, and 'Icicle' speedwell form the backbone for this moonlight theme garden.

all-white flowers and plants with silver or variegated foliage. It was quite a pastime to go into the garden on a moonlit night and enjoy the eerie glow of the white flowers and unusual foliage.

Planning a moonlight garden is just like planning any other garden, but you will be choosing plants particularly for the foliage and white flowers. It is easy to get carried away worrying about the details of color, so remember to pay attention to the ultimate height and spread of the plants. The plant list included here suggests both perennial and annual plants, as well as herbs and flowers for you to choose from.

PERENNIALS IN THE KITCHEN GARDEN

Perennials plants and entire perennial beds can be worked into the plan for the kitchen garden if care is taken during the planning stages. Perennials will last in your garden beds for three years or more. Some of them will thrive for as long as twenty years. Getting to know the individual personality of each perennial is enjoyable to most gardeners, and is an essential part of working with this diverse group of plants.

In the following pages you will find general cultural information and guidelines regarding perennials, as well as some profiles of outstanding perennials for your kitchen garden.

GENERAL TIPS

Perennial plants differ in their likes and dislikes, but there are some general rules to growing them successfully. The first rule is to learn the habit and needs of the plants you are planning to grow—among the plants you have chosen may be one that is an exception to these rules.

Perennials can be started from seed, but this takes an extraordinary amount of patience and is not recommended to beginning gardeners. Most folks do best (and get

results much more quickly) when they purchase more mature container-grown plants.

When choosing perennials you must pay attention to the climate zones that set the geographical range in which the plant can grow. Most perennials have specific tolerances to how much winter cold or summer heat they can withstand. Learn what zone you live in (see page 138) and choose plants accordingly.

When you choose perennials, try to plan for a succession of bloom. Most perennials have a bloom time of only three to six weeks. Planning well assures that something is in bloom all season long.

SOIL

Most perennials must have well-drained soil. Soggy soil or standing water damages the root system of the plant, and in most cases will eventually kill it. Many perennials are able to thrive in a leaner soil than you will have prepared for your kitchen garden, but there are exceptions that prefer richer soil. Generally speaking, if you have prepared your beds according to the information in this book you should be all set to grow perennials successfully for many years.

WATER

Once your perennials are established in garden beds, they will need less water than vegetables demand. Usually your plants will tell you if they are in need of water—you will see signs of wilting. Too much water can make your plants leggy and weak. Watering is usually necessary only when young plants are getting established, during dry periods, or when you notice wilting foliage. Water deeply or do not water at all.

PLANTING STRATEGIES

Perennials look their best when planted in groups of three or more. Informal groupings of plants look much more attractive than plants set out in rows. Try to plant contrasting foliages next to each other in the bed. The foliage will be evident all season long, and if your plants are well chosen, foliage contrast can be as attractive as flowers. Take care to keep taller plants from blocking the shorter plants from view.

Container-grown plants can be planted at any time during the growing season; of course if they are planted in the hottest, driest part of the summer, they will need daily watering until they are established. Perennials appreciate a drink of water when they are planted—fill the hole with water and allow it to drain out, then plant as usual. Water the new plants in thoroughly.

PERENNIAL PLANT PROFILES

The plants listed in these profiles are tried-and-true perennials. I have chosen them because they are relatively small and neat, require little maintenance, have a longer bloom time than most perennials, offer beautiful foliage and flowers, and are adaptable to a wide range of conditions.

CORAL BELLS (HEUCHERA X BRIZOIDES)—HARDY TO ZONE 4

Coral bells are an old-fashioned perennial. They have interesting, nearly evergreen foliage that arises from a thick, fleshy root. Even when they are not in flower, their foliage is beautifully ornamental. It is sometimes crinkled, usually mottled with silver or red overtones, and may have distinct zonal patterns depending on the variety. Some varieties have deep burgundy foliage.

Coral bells begin to bloom in May in northern areas, providing early food for hummingbirds. The bell-shaped flowers are held on short stalks, and the flower color ranges from snow white to delicate pink to fiery red.

Thanks to good care and maintenance, this beautifully planted garden brims with healthy flowers and herbs, to the delight of this fortunate feline.

They bloom nearly all season long, withholding flowers only in the hottest weather.

Coral bells have a lovely demeanor in the garden, forming distinct mounds of foliage of 12 to 18 inches (30 to 45cm) across that never overwhelm nearby plants. They require very little maintenance, though mature plants may need to be divided occasionally. During the winter months the nearly evergreen leaves may become burned by the cold, dry air. In spring, trim off such damaged leaves and allow new foliage to regrow. Coral bells will thrive in well-drained average soil in sun or partial shade.

DWARF BLEEDING HEART (DICENTRA EXIMIA)—HARDY TO ZONE 4

Dwarf bleeding heart is one of the easiest, most care-free perennials to be found. The deeply divided, ferny foliage emerges from the ground as soon as the soil warms, and flowers are not far behind. The foliage is a blue-green color and makes a nice contrast to other foliage in the garden.

The flowers are pink, and are heart-shaped, like other bleeding heart species. A lovely white-flowered cultivar, called 'Alba', can sometimes be found and is equally pleasing. Bloom time is from early spring through autumn. As with many such plants, blooming falls off in the hottest weather and resumes with vigor in late summer and autumn.

Dwarf bleeding heart needs no maintenance to speak of. Spent flowers may by pruned off, but if you desire seedlings from the parent plant, leave the flowers in place. The plants will self-sow, but not enough to become a nuisance. The foliage dies back to the ground each autumn and seldom needs pruning.

Dwarf bleeding heart is reliable for many years, and does not need to be divided.

OPPOSITE, TOP: 'Chatterbox' coral bells display their miniature flowers atop long slender stems. OPPOSITE, BOTTOM: No cottage garden would be complete without the old-fashioned charm of bleeding hearts. LEFT: As if competing for your attention, an attractive mix of flowers—including 'Monte Rosa' lilies, foxgloves, bellflowers, and cabbage roses—burst forth from a garden bed.

RIGHT: Nature's bounty fills this flower basket with blooms for the drying shed. OPPOSITE, TOP: Dried roses, sea lavender, statice, herb foliage, and globe amaranth flowers combine to great effect in this gorgeous wreath. OPPOSITE, BOTTOM: Many flowers dry easily if tied in loose bundles and hung to dry. Here roses, delphiniums, and pink pokers dry side by side.

An Everlasting Wreath From Your Garden

What better way to remember the gentle summer months than with a wreath fashioned from the flowers you grew in your everlasting garden. The simple and easy-to-follow instructions below will help you create this beautiful wreath, and you will be pleasantly surprised by how little time it takes.

You will need:

Coat hanger

Wire cutters

Floral tape

Florist's wire

Glue gun and glue sticks

Assorted dried herb foliage or baby's breath

Assorted dried flowers

1. Cut the hook end of the coat hanger off using wire cutters. Using the remaining coat hanger wire, make a circlet of wire about 6 or 7 inches (15 to 18cm) in diameter. Overlap the ends to form a circle—this will be the form for your wreath.

2. Wrap florist's tape around the wreath base until all the wire is covered. This will prevent the florist's wire from slipping as you create the base of flowers or foliage that will form the background of your wreath arrangement.

3. You may use catnip, sage, or lavender foliage for the base or you may combine them. Sweet Annie flowers work well too, as does baby's breath. Use what you have dried from your garden—they will all look lovely. Bring the dried flowers and herbs to your work station.

4. Make small bundles of foliage or flowers—about 4 inches (10cm) long is good. Affix them to the wire base by wrapping the florist's wire around the bottom of the bundle and the wreath form. Make sure that each bundle is securely in place. Start in one spot and work your way around the wreath in one direction.

5. Make another bundle and place it on the wreath form so that it just covers the stems of the first bundle, then wire it to the form. Continue wiring in this fashion until all of the form is covered. When you reach the end, cut off the florist's wire, leaving about 6 inches (15cm) on the form. Use this to make a hanging loop on the back of the wreath.

6. Next, you will be adding accent flowers to the wreath base. You can use small straw flowers, ammobium, gomphrena, or any others you wish, as long as the size of the flower stays in proportion with the size of the wreath. Using a glue gun, glue the larger flowers on and then fill between them with smaller flowers. Leave enough of the base material showing through to look attractive.

7. Lay the wreath on a flat surface until the materials have dried sufficiently.

It thrives in all but the poorest or soggiest soils in full sun or light shade.

SEDUM, STONECROP *(SEDUM* SPP.)— HARDY TO ZONE 3

In this genus of plants it is difficult to choose a favorite. All have succulent fleshy foliage and many thrive in hot, dry soils.

There are many species of summer-blooming sedums. Most are less than 1 foot (30cm) in height and some are most commonly used as groundcovers. Even among those that spread, none are difficult to move or eradicate from the landscape. *Sedum spurium* 'Dragon's Blood' has red-tinted foliage and makes a nice groundcover. Other good groundcover types are *Sedum acre* and *Sedum rupestre* 'Blue Spruce'.

Sedum spurium 'Tricolor' and *Sedum kamtschaticum* are summer-blooming sedums that are more wisely used as specimen plants. 'Tricolor' has green, white, and red foliage, while *S. kamtschaticum* has deep green foliage topped by brilliant yellow flowers.

Still another taller group of sedums blooms in the autumn. This group is prized not only for their foliage but for the nice display of flat-topped autumn flowers they provide. *Sedum* 'Indian Chief' and 'Autumn Joy' are two commonly found varieties. Their red flowers contrast beautifully with the blue-green foliage, and they form large, well-mannered clumps that can be divided every few years. The cultivar 'Vera Jameson' has reddish foliage all season long.

Some sedums die back to the ground each autumn, and some are evergreen. None need anything but the most minimal trimming to remove last year's foliage or flowers. Sedums will perform best full sun in hot dry soils, but are widely adaptable to all but soggy conditions.

Interplanted vegetables and flowers create a patchwork of color in this sprawling country garden. A stroll through the garden is a virtual feast for the senses; flowers delight the eye, scents arise from blooms and herbs, foliage fuzzy and silky caresses the skin, and fresh vegetables and fruits just wait to be tasted.

THREADLEAF COREOPSIS *(COREOPSIS VERTICILLATA)* HARDY TO ZONE 3

Threadleaf coreopsis is a spectacular summer- and fall-blooming perennial. The foliage looks very delicate and fine, but these plants are tough.

The cultivars 'Golden Showers' and 'Moonbeam' thrive in full sun in nearly any well-drained soil. 'Golden Showers' is golden yellow, and is the most likely cultivar to need staking. 'Moonbeam' has a profusion of lemon yellow, 1-inch (2.5cm), daisylike flowers that dance on the top of each stem. It blooms from midsummer through autumn. 'Zagreb' also gives a generous bloom of golden yellow, 1-inch (2.5cm) flowers, but blooms a bit later.

C. rosea, a close relative of *C. verticillata,* also blooms with a profusion of daisylike flowers about ¾ inch (2cm) across. This plant thrives in a more damp soil in light shade.

These coreopsis species attain a height of 15 to 24 inches (38 to 60cm) and form good-sized clumps quickly. If they overspread their allotted space, they are easy to remove. They can be divided yearly in most cases. Coreopsis need only have the withered foliage removed from the plant in autumn or spring.

RIGHT: The flowers of threadleaf coreopsis are variations on the daisy shape, but these top-performing plants are studded with flowers and reward you with a long bloom time. OPPOSITE: 'Special Mixture' coreopsis lends its cheerful flowers to this field of blooms.

fruits large and small

Fruits add healthy food, beauty, and grace to the kitchen garden. The variety of fruits that can be grown in your garden is influenced largely by the area in which you live. In some areas citrus fruits, kiwis, persimmons, and other exotic fruits can be grown, but those of us in colder regions will have to be satisfied with more common fare.

This chapter is designed as an introduction to growing fruits at home. Because pest problems are prevalent and differ for each type of fruit, this chapter does not discuss them except in a very general sense. For more information, check the resource guide on page 136 for some excellent books that focus on this very large topic.

From this chapter you will get an idea of the effort it takes to grow fruit trees at home, for this is often a time-consuming endeavor. Small fruits, on the other hand, are easier to grow and can make lovely additions to the kitchen garden. This chapter will also serve as a reintroduction to some of the small fruits that have been nearly forgotten by agriculture.

Tart pie cherries are one of the easier fruits to grow. You can freeze them for pies if you don't eat them before they reach the freezer!

STANDARD FRUITING TREES

Fruit trees have an allure that is irresistible to many gardeners. They add a great deal to the landscape, especially when they are in flower or fruit.

As appealing as they are, fruit trees are rather labor intensive. They present pest problems that must be addressed on a timely basis, or you will not be satisfied with the results. It is inevitable that in most areas the trees will need spraying, and you will have the added expense of spray and a sprayer. For this reason, most gardeners should think through the commitment it will take to grow fruit trees in a kitchen garden.

SELECTING FRUIT TREE VARIETIES

When selecting fruit tree varieties, you cannot be too careful. There are hundreds of cultivars on the market, and the trees you choose should be well suited to your growing area. For help in selecting specific varieties well adapted to your area, contact the Department of Agriculture, who will put you in touch with the State Experimental Station nearest you. These experimental stations carry out field trials and testing on new and old varieties that show promise for agricultural purposes. These local extension offices also may have pamphlets available with detailed cultural information regarding each type of fruit. These publications are usually offered at a minimal cost to the public. The extension service also should have a list of recommended varieties for your area.

Most gardeners have precious little space for fruit trees. For this reason most opt to grow dwarf or semidwarf varieties. Be sure to check the spacing requirements for the trees you are contemplating for your garden, and decide

beforehand whether or not you have room to accommodate them. Fruit trees that are crowded are seldom attractive or as productive as they otherwise would be.

PLANTING FRUIT TREES

The adage "dig a ten dollar hole for a one dollar tree" never rang truer, as fruit trees are quite particular about their soil requirements. It pays to take your time and plant the trees correctly.

Fruit trees prefer well-drained soil in full sun; if your soil is soggy, the trees may languish. If the soil has been prepared according to the information in Chapter 1, you are well on your way to having healthy trees.

The following describes a good old-fashioned method for planting fruit trees. Follow it religiously and you will be rewarded with earlier yield and good production.

TIMING

Fruit trees are best planted when they are dormant in early spring. Order early in the year so that the nursery can ship your trees before the buds start to open. If you miss this planting time, wait until the following year. Planting

OPPOSITE: Luscious oranges are easily grown in warm climates. There is nothing like the taste of a ripe orange fresh off the tree. ABOVE: If you can't grow citrus fruits such as these lemons out of doors, check your local florist or greenhouse for varieties that will do well in pots. The trees can be set out in the summer and will produce small fruits reliably.

Trees grown as espaliers take up less space and produce higher-quality fruit, but the process is a demanding one. The desired branches must be trained to a support, and unwanted shoots must constantly be pinched back. In areas with long hot summers, where growth is rampant, this can be a daunting task. Still, it may be well worth learning the art of espaliering if space is limited.

late in the season almost always leads to disappointing results.

PLANTING STRATEGY

Dig a hole 3 feet (90cm) deep and 3 feet across, piling the soil to the side of the hole. Make a mixture of compost, composted manure, peat moss, and topsoil (if your garden soil is good you can substitute it for the topsoil), mixing all the ingredients well. Add to this mixture 3 pounds (1.4kg) of rock phosphate.

Remove the tree from the wrapping and remove any string or wire from the limbs. Prune off any damaged or broken limbs. Examine the root system and prune off any damaged roots. Fill the hole with the soil mix you have made until it is about half full. Place a large rock in the hole or make a mound of soil in the center, then place the roots over this. Check the graft union on the stem of the tree—the graft should be above the soil line. Add more soil before placing the tree if needed. Make a mound in the center of the hole or place the roots back on the rock, then spread the roots so that they fan out downward in all directions. Fill the hole with the remaining soil mixture and firm it with your foot. Leave a slight depression in the soil near the base of the tree so that a little extra rain will collect there to water the tree.

Be certain to give your fruit trees plenty of room in which to grow. Mail-order sources will give spacing requirements for fruit trees that are dwarf, semidwarf, or of standard size. Never skimp on these space requirements.

If you live in a windy area, you may want to stake your fruit trees to keep them upright until the roots take hold. Fruit trees should be watered thoroughly once a week the first growing season. All fruit trees need pruning in the years to follow. Again, your local agricultural station should have brochures detailing the best pruning techniques.

PREVENTIVE MAINTENANCE

A good preventive against problems during the growing season is dormant oil spray. Dormant oil spray is applied while the trees are still dormant in late winter or very early spring. It literally smothers potential problems such as overwintering pests or pest eggs laid in the bark. Dormant oil spray is considered nontoxic.

FRUIT TREES FOR THE KITCHEN GARDEN

APPLES

Apples are among the most popular fruit trees to grow at home, and varieties exist for a wide range of purposes, including baking and making cider.

OPPOSITE: Apples fresh off the tree help celebrate the autumn season. Consider planting an unusual or heirloom variety in your kitchen garden. ABOVE: These apples have been wrapped with care, and are ready to store or ship as gifts. Many varieties of apples can be placed in cold storage for use throughout the winter months.

Apple trees are not self-pollinating, so at least two (three are even better) varieties are needed to ensure good pollination of the blossoms. If you have a small yard, apples can take up all the space you have because of these requirements. If there are apple trees close by, they might aid in the pollination of your trees.

Apples are susceptible to many pest problems and need close attention during the growing season. Coddling moth, apple fly, scab, rust, and fire blight all affect apples

APRICOTS

This luscious fruit can be an elusive crop for the backyard grower. Apricot trees need quite a bit of room in which to grow—up to 25 feet (7.5m). Apricots are early bloomers, so in northern areas freezing weather often kills the flower buds. There are also some varieties of apricots that are termed "shy bloomers." Check varieties very carefully before ordering nursery stock to be certain the trees will do well in your area.

While many apricots are self-pollinating, some are not, so check catalogs carefully before ordering. In warm areas the trees need a period of cold weather in order for flower buds to develop properly the following season. Apricots can be damaged by fungal problems such as brown rot and blackheart. Insects that bore into fruit tree bark can also become problematic. If these problems occur, prune off and burn any affected wood.

SWEET AND SOUR CHERRIES

Sweet and sour cherries are often found in backyard gardens. Sweet cherry trees generally take more time before they will set fruit. Sour cherries will start to bear quite early in life and are easier to grow, but the trees may be shorter lived.

Most cherries are not self-pollinating, so two or more varieties are needed for reliable fruit set. Even self-pollinating types will set a better crop if another variety is nearby. Sweet cherries pollinate other sweet cherries, and sour cherries pollinate other sour cherries.

Antique Apples

If you want to grow apples, consider a historical variety, many of which are superior in taste to what is grown for today's marketplace. Antique apples are rarely available at markets and are mainly grown by backyard gardeners. Although we think of apples as an autumn crop, some antique varieties ripen by July and some as late as November. The reason for this was simple—with no refrigeration to help store the fruit, such varieties extended the season in which fresh fruit could be enjoyed. Certain apples were grown specifically for cider, pies, or their keeping ability.

Below is a list of a few of the antique apple varieties available and their chief characteristics:

'Wolf River'—Huge apples from the banks of the Wolf River in Wisconsin. Very productive.

'Snow Apple' ('Fameuse')—Apple from France grown in North America in the early 1600s. Tender and spicy with snow white flesh that is sometimes streaked with red.

'Dutchess of Oldenburg'—Originated in Russia and grown in North America for more than 150 years. Somewhat resistant to disease. Flat fruit with red striping; ripens August to September.

'Lodi'—Light green fruit ripens in late July to August. Holds its texture well; good sauce apple.

'Golden Russet'—A favorite in colonial America; primarily a cider apple.

'Pound Sweet'—Fruits over a pound (0.5kg) are the norm for this tree; light green to yellow in color. Some say this is the best baking apple there is; ripens in September.

'Spitzenburg'—Thomas Jefferson's favorite apple; excellent for eating canning and cooking. Good keeper.

'Sheepnose'—Sometimes called 'Black Gilliflower'; originated in Connecticut. Fruit is ribbed and deep red, nearly black; baking and dessert apple.

Sweet and sour cherries have several pest problems. Plum curculio is usually to blame for worms in cherries. Birds can be a serious problem come harvest time, and netting may be the only way to deter them. Tent caterpillars also show a preference for cherry trees. The most serious threat to sour cherries is black knot, a lethal fungal disease that shows itself as a black canker or growth on the tree. This growth should be pruned off the tree—taking the entire branch is best—as early in the season as possible. Once black knot shows itself, it is often fatal to the tree. Offending wood should be burned or

OPPOSITE: Antique apple varieties are indelibly linked with our history. Sadly, many are unavailable to buy fresh, but trees are still available from specialty nurseries.

removed from the property entirely or it can infect other trees.

GRAPES

Today many grape varieties are available for the kitchen gardener to try. Wine grapes and table grapes are both relatively easy to grow. Their most stringent requirement is a system of support, for the vines must be trained to it. Everyone who grows grapes has a way of overcoming this, from arbors to trellises to pergolas. You will want to study several solutions and choose the one that seems best for your garden situation.

Most grape varieties are self-pollinating. Grapes produce fruit on this year's wood, so grapes need regular pruning to keep the vines productive and under control. This pruning is done in early spring before the buds begin to break dormancy.

The most common problem that grapes endure is mummy berry, which is caused by a fungus. Affected grapes look like mummies— hard and all shriveled up. As soon as they appear to be affected, remove such grapes from the vine. Copper-based sprays may be of help in battling this problem. Japanese beetles feed heavily on the leaves in the summer.

PEACHES

Surprisingly, good crops of peaches can be grown in all but the most severe climates. Choice of variety is paramount when choosing nursery stock, so consult your nearest agricultural station for suggestions.

Peaches resent being transplanted, so most manuals recommend that the top be cut back about 25 percent to lessen the stress on the tree.

Peaches are subject to several problems, including plum curculio, bacterial leaf spot, peach leaf curl, and peach tree borer. Peach leaf curl is caused by ants carrying aphids up the tree to the leaves. The aphids feed on the leaves and the ants go back to harvest the honeydew that the aphids secrete. It is easier to stop the ants with a sticky trap barrier on the trunk than it is to spray the tree.

PEARS

Pears are a wonderful fruit for the kitchen garden, and pear trees are much more tolerant of adverse soil conditions than other fruit trees. There are several types of pears widely available today. These include eating pears, seckel pears, winter pears, and Asian pears. Seckel pears are small and extremely sweet. Winter pears often ripen very late in the season—sometimes as late as November. They store well and develop a sweet flavor in storage. Asian pears have a crisp texture and are reportedly more disease-resistant than other pears.

Pear trees are not self-pollinating, and so require two varieties in order to set fruit. Like other fruit trees they are susceptible to many pests and diseases. Fire blight is the most prevalent disease and is often fatal. So susceptible to fire blight is the Bartlett pear, that I would never recommend growing it in your garden. Pear scab, pear leaf spot, sooty mold, and sooty blotch all can affect pears.

PLUMS

Two types of plums can be grown in the kitchen garden—Japanese plums and prune plums. Prune plums are either eaten fresh or

OPPOSITE, CLOCKWISE FROM TOP LEFT: Pears should not be allowed to ripen on the tree, but should instead finish ripening in storage. Grapes grown over an arbor are a favorite of many gardeners. Just-picked peaches fill the air with their incredible aroma. Juicy and delicious, plums are a delicacy eaten fresh from the tree and are old favorites for jellies and jams. **RIGHT:** Many pear varieties are available for the home orchard. Pears trees will often bear bumper crops in the home garden.

used for canning, while Japanese plums are strictly for eating fresh.

Plum trees are susceptible to many of the same problems as other fruits. Plum curculio, scale, brown rot, and peach tree borer are all to be expected. In addition to these things, plum trees must be watched for any sign of black knot, a fungal disease that is usually fatal a few years after it becomes obvious. When black knot is spotted, the offending branch should be removed and burned or removed from the property entirely as early in the season as possible, or it could infect other trees. Birds are often a problem come harvest time, especially for Japanese plums.

SMALL FRUITS FOR THE KITCHEN GARDEN

Small fruits are much easier to grow than fruit trees, and are reliable producers in the kitchen garden. Small fruits are also less labor-intensive; they have fewer pest problems and they demand much less space than standard fruit trees. If you have never grown fruit of any kind, the delicious small fruits discussed here are an excellent starting place.

ABOVE: No room for a strawberry bed? Try raising them in pots, but be sure to keep the soil evenly moist. OPPOSITE: A good space-saving method for growing strawberries is on a specially designed pole. Many plants can be grown in a small space and the berries are easy to harvest.

In this section you'll find recommendations for growing these garden jewels. An emphasis has been put on keeping the labor to a minimum.

STRAWBERRIES

Strawberries are the fruit of choice for most kitchen gardens—it is hard to equal the flavor of the berries that you grow in your own yard. Strawberry plants are usually sold in lots of twenty-five plants, which will give most gardeners all the fresh berries they want.

Strawberries like a rich, moisture-retentive soil that is somewhat acidic. Plants should be planted in early spring and can be set 18 inches (45cm) apart in rows about 3 feet (90cm) apart. The first year, remove the blooms so that the plants can put all their energy into producing runners. These runners should be allowed to spread and fill in the bed. The following season all the plants will bear fruit.

There are many labor-intensive ways in which these berries can be grown from this point forward, but I prefer a simple approach. The beds will have filled in with runners and will have produced the first true crop of berries in the summer of their second full year in your garden. They will continue to grow and produce runners to expand the bed further, overrunning their allotted space. Sooner or later, the plants that have produced for several seasons will become less productive. Rather than destroying all of the runners, you can use them to gradually replace the original plants in the bed.

When the berry patch loses productivity, it is time to reorder and begin a fresh bed in another location. This cycle usually runs its course in five to seven years. This low-maintenance method saves a lot of fussing with creating replacement beds and keeping the berry patch up to impossibly high standards. If you

decide this approach is not for you, you can always buy new plants to start the beds anew every other year or so.

Strawberry beds are more enjoyable during the harvest season if a light mulch of straw or pine straw is used to keep soil off the berries. The most serious pests are slugs and birds.

CANE FRUITS

Cane fruits include raspberries, blackberries, and black caps, or black raspberries. In most areas of North America they are vigorous and easy to grow. Choosing the right variety for your growing conditions is important, especially if you live in a warm climate.

Cane fruits should be grown on a site a bit removed from the kitchen garden. This is because they do not stay put—new canes will grow from the base of the plants and work their way through the garden. Once they have started, they are very difficult to stop. A row of cane fruits can be grown 10 to 12 feet (3 to 3.5m) away from the garden; leave the space between planted in grass, and any offending canes will be mowed down and discouraged regularly.

There are many fussy ways to grow these fruits by placing them on trellis systems to keep the canes upright. My preference is to let the canes grow naturally. Spring pruning consists of removing any weak or dead canes. Right after the canes have finished bearing, you can remove those that bore fruit by cutting them right to the ground. This allows the plant to put all its energy into the canes that will produce fruit next season. If the bed becomes too wide to pick comfortably, you can cut it to the ground and let it grow back selectively.

OPPOSITE: Raspberries grow together with asparagus and poppies on the edge of a woodland. ABOVE: Vibrant red raspberries and blueberries reward gardeners who have prepared the soil well and kept plants evenly moist as they set fruit.

Fruit worms can sometimes attack the berries themselves, but are easily controlled with rotenone/pyrethrum spray.

CURRANTS AND GOOSEBERRIES

Currants and gooseberries are little known by most North American gardeners, which is a pity because they are the easiest, most care-free fruits that you can grow at home and are prime candidates for use in sauces, jams, and pies.

Currants and gooseberries have also suffered in popularity because they have been identified as a host for white pine blister rust, a disease of the white pine tree. They are still banned from shipment to certain areas. To be safe, currants and gooseberries should not be planted within 900 feet (275m) of white pines.

Currants are a joy in the kitchen garden. Their tart flavor and gorgeous color should pique the interest of anyone who enjoys cooking. Currants come in three colors—red, white, and black. Black currants have been used mainly dried as a substitute for raisins, but are seldom available. Red or white currants are more widely available.

Currants establish themselves quickly—their ultimate size is 4 to 5 feet (1.2 to 1.5) high, and they should be planted no closer than 4 feet (1.2) apart. They are not fussy about the soil they will grow in as long as it is not overly dry or overly wet. Full sun is recommended, but they will do reasonably well in light shade. Currants are self-pollinating, so only one plant is needed to produce a crop.

Currants are beautiful in the landscape. The foliage is quite interesting and appears early in the season. They bloom early as well, and feature small dangling clusters of light yellow flowers. The flowers are followed in midsummer by the gemlike fruit.

Currants are sometimes bothered by currant worm, which appears on the young tender foliage. This pest is easily controlled with pyrethrum, but take care not to spray the flowers or bees that pollinate them.

The only pruning that is necessary for currants is to prune out ⅓ of the old wood each spring. This helps to keep the plants productive.

Gooseberries are similar to currants in many ways, except that the fruit is much larger and the plants themselves sport thorns. They are of value in the kitchen for pies, jellies, jams, and marmalades. Some cultivars have tart fruits and some have sweeter fruits that are more suited to eating fresh.

Gooseberries vary in size and shape according to variety. Like currants, they will eventually grow to about 4 feet (1.2) in height and should be planted 4 feet (1.2) apart. They grow quickly and bear fruit very easily. Gosseberries do best in full sun but will tolerate light shade, and are not particular about soil unless it is overly dry or overly wet. Gooseberries are self-pollinating, so only one plant is necessary to produce fruit.

Gooseberries are highly ornamental in the landscape, setting foliage and flowering early in the season. Fruits are borne in small clusters and are about the size of a grape, depending on variety. They are sometimes bothered by currant worm, which usually affects the young, tender foliage. Currant worm can be controlled with pyrethrum, but take care not to spray flowers or pollinating bees.

Because of their thorns, gooseberries should not be planted in confined spaces. They do make a nice impenetrable hedge in the right location. Prune out ⅓ of the old wood each spring to keep plants healthy and productive.

Gooseberry–Kumquat Marmalade

This marmalade sparkles like a gem and tastes even better. The tartness of the gooseberries is a perfect complement for the sweet favor of kumquats. This delicious spread is excellent with meats or poultry as well as on an English muffin.

You will need:

2 cups kumquats, seeded and chopped fine

7 cups sugar

½ cup (125ml) or so water

1 package fruit pectin powder

Seed kumquats. Stem gooseberries and place with kumquats in a food processor fitted with the knife blade. Pulse until the two fruits are chopped but not pureed. Use 5½ to 6 cups of this mixture, adding a little extra water if necessary.

Stir the powdered pectin into the mixture and bring to a boil for one minute in a large heavy pan. Add all the sugar and bring back to a full boil for one minute. Can in self-sealing jars and place in a hot water bath for 10 minutes.

OPPOSITE: Gooseberry bushes take up little space in the garden and are prolific bearers. RIGHT: Currants are tart and juicy—and are a delight for the creative cook. Enough currants can be grown on one or two bushes to provide for a family of four.

BLUEBERRIES

The key to growing blueberries is twofold—both patience and acidic soil are needed. Blueberries are slow growers, so securing a crop will take several seasons. Soil also plays a key role in their development.

Blueberries need acidic soil—a pH of 4.5 to 5.5 is the best growing range. They also require good drainage and are often killed by soggy soil. Unless your soil is naturally acidic you will need to treat it to bring it up to snuff. For the health of your plants the best way to do this is through an organic approach.

When the shrubs are planted, dig a hole a 2 to 3 feet (60 to 90cm) wide and 2 feet (60cm) deep. Replace one half the soil with peat moss and use this mixture to backfill the hole. Be certain to plant blueberries at the same depth to which they were planted in the nursery container. Firm the soil around the roots and water the shrubs well.

To keep the soil acidic, use a mulch of pine straw. Common advice is to douse the roots with a solution of commercially prepared soil acidifier or sulphur, but I do not recommend this tactic. Instead, a good layer (about 3 to 6 feet [1 to 1.8m]) of pine straw mulch will enrich the soil and keep it at a good pH for the plants.

Blueberries do best in full sun. They need little pruning, except to remove dead or weak wood each spring. Occasionally, tent caterpillars invade blueberries. They should be removed and destroyed as soon as they become evident. Blueberries are attractive forage for many types of birds, so you may find it necessary to protect them with netting to get a harvest.

LEFT: Blueberries mature in stages rather than all at once. Pick carefully to avoid disturbing those that have not yet ripened. OPPOSITE: Don't forget to enjoy the fruits of your labor, here with a simple yet glorious breakfast.

SUTTONS SEEDS

GLORIOUS FRAGRA

Pea Feltham First (Early)

Extremely widely grown, smooth seeded variety. The earliest spring sowing variety to harvest. It is dwarf so does not need sticks. Hgt. 45cm (18in).

INSTRUCTIONS FOR SOWING:

Peas prefer a deep rich, moist soil which has had plenty of well rotted manure or compost dug in the previous autumn winter. Commence sowing in early spring once the soil has started to warm up and is easily worked. Sowing can be carried out until early summer, and an autumn sowing made for overwintering in mild winter areas. Sow at 10 day intervals for succession, making flat bottomed drills 5cm (2in) deep, 15-20cm (6-8in) wide. Place 2 rows of seeds 5-8cm (2-3in) apart both ways and replace the soil. Allow 46cm (18in) between each drill. Keep the rows weeded and once the plants are 8-10cm (3-4in) tall twiggy sticks for support can be provided although this is not essential. Give water twice a week during flowering and pod development to ensure a good and heavier crop. Commence picking when the pods have started to swell. Regular picking will also improve the cropping flavour of the peas.

sources

Over the years I have ordered just about every type of gardening supply available. Everyone has their favorite sources for tools, seeds, and so on. Do not neglect specialty garden stores that may be located in your area—these are often a good source of hard-to-find items.

Here you'll find sources for the items discussed in this book. I have tried to list as many companies as possible, but no doubt there are many that I have overlooked. Several of the companies listed here supply more than one item, and so will be listed under more than one heading.

Some gardeners complain about getting too many catalogs in the mail. Although lots of junk mail can be disturbing, I prefer to have catalogs on hand that offer solutions to my problems as they arise, and you might too. Happy hunting!

UNUSUAL FLOWER AND VEGETABLE SEEDS

Thompson and Morgan Inc
P.O. Box 1308
Jackson, New Jersey 08527-0308
1-800-274-7333
Many seeds of plants grown in Europe and the
U.K.

The Fragrant Path
P.O.Box 328
Fort Calhoun, Nebraska 68023
Specialty is seeds from fragrant flowers, vines,
and shrubs.

Prairie Oak Seeds
P.O.Box 382
Maryville, MO 64468-0382
Wide selection of everlastings.

Abundant Life Seed Foundation
P.O.Box 772
Port Townsend, Washington 98368
Open-pollinated vegetable seeds; this catalog
carries no hybrid seed.

J.L. Hudson, Seedsman
Star Route 2, Box 337
La Honda, California 94020
Unusual herb and flower seed, zapotics and
heirloom vegetable seed.

Nichols Garden Nursery
1190 North Pacific Highway
Albany, Oregon 97321-4580
541-928-9280
Herb seeds, unusual vegetable seeds, "fill your
own" tea bags.
Seeds of Change

P.O.Box 15700
Santa Fe, New Mexico 87506-5700
Certified organic vegetable herb and flower
seed, many varieties endemic in southwestern
culture.

FLOWER AND VEGETABLE SEEDS

Sheperd's Garden Seeds
30 Irene Street
Torrington, Connecticut 06790
860-482-3638
Gourmet vegetable seeds, herb and flower seed,
emphasis on flavor.

Park Seed Company
1 Parkton Ave.
Greenwood, South Carolina 29647-0001
864-223-7333
Wide selection of all types of seeds.

Stokes Seeds Inc.
Box 548
Buffalo, New York 14240-0548
716-695-6980
Vegetable, flower, and herb seeds; vegetable
varieties specifically selected to do well in
northern climates.

Johnny's Selected Seeds
Foss Hill Road
Albion, Maine 04910-9731
207-437-4301
Vegetable, flower and herb seeds; unusual vari-
eties, many specifically selected for New
England and northern climates.

J.W. Jung Seed Co.
Randolph, Wisconsin 53957
800-247-5864
Vegetable, flower, and herb seeds with a flair
for old standby varieties.

Harris Seeds
60 Saginaw Drive
P.O.Box 22960
Rochester, New York 14692-2960
800-514-4441
Vegetable, flower, and herb seeds with a good
mix of old and new varieties.

Pinetree Garden Seeds
Box 300
New Gloucester, Maine 04260
207-926-3400
Small reasonably priced seed packets for the
home garden.

UNUSUAL PERENNIAL PLANTS

Forest Farm
990 Tetherow Rd.
Williams, Oregon 97544-9599

Heronswood Nursery
7530 288th St. NE
Kingston, Washington 98346

Shady Oaks Nursery
112 10th Avenue S.E.
Waseca, Minnesota 56093
Specializes in hostas and perennials for shady
situations.

White Flower Farm
P.O.Box 50
Litchfield, Connecticut 06759-0050
800-503-9624

UNUSUAL HERBS

Sandy Mush Herb Nursery
316 Surrett Cove Road
Leicester, North Carolina 28748-9622

FRUIT STOCK

Henry Leuthhardt Nurseries, Inc.
Montauk Highway, Box 666
East Moriches, New York 11940-0666
516-878-1387
Unusual fruits of all kinds.

Miller Nurseries
5060 West Lake Road
Canandaigua, New York 14424
800-836-9630
Rare and choice varieties of fruit tree stock, antique apples.

Hartman's Plantation
310 60th Street P.O. Box E
Grand Junction, Michigan 49056
616-253-4281
Rare edible fruits and ornamental plants, kiwis; blueberries are their specialty.

Raintree Nursery
391 Butts Road
Morton, Washington 98356
206-496-6400
Unusual fruits, kiwi, nut trees, citrus trees, paw paw, persimmons, antique apples, and other edibles for the landscape.

Northwoods Retail Nursery
27635 S Oglesby Rd.
Canby, Oregon 97013
503-266-5432
Unusual fruits, antique apples, paw paw, nuts, ornamentals, pomegranate, citrus trees, figs, small fruits, and kiwi.

J.W. Jung Seed Company
Randolph, Wisconsin 53975
800-247-5864
Standard fruits, antique apples, small fruits for northern areas.

Burford Brothers
P.O. Box 367
Monroe, Virginia 24574
804-929-4950

Bear Creek Nursery
P.O. Box 411
Northport, Washington 99157
509-732-6219

GENERAL GARDEN SUPPLIES AND TOOLS:

Lee Valley Tools LTD
P.O. Box 1780
Ogdensburg, New York 213669-0490

Gardeners Supply Company
128 Intervale Road
Burlington, Vermont 05401
800-863-1700

Plow and Hearth
P.O.Box 5000
Madison, Virginia 22727-1500

The Necessary Trading Company
One Nature's Way
New Castle, Virginia 24127-0305
Environmentally friendly pest solutions and sprays, beneficial insects.

Gardens Alive
5100 Schenley Place
Lawrenceburg, Indiana 47025
812-537-8650
Environmentally friendly pest controls and solutions.

The Kinsman Company
River Road
Point Pleasant, Pennsylvania 18950

A.M. Leonard, Inc.
241 Fox Drive
P.O. Box 816
Piqua, Ohio 45356

DEER NETTING

Benner's Gardens, Inc.
6974 Upper York Road
New Hope, Pennsylvania 18938
800-753-4660

MISCELLANEOUS

United States Department of Agriculture can be reached at 202-720-8732

For additional information concerning organic pest and disease control consult:

CANADA

Corn Hill Nursery Ltd.
RR 5
Petitcodiac, New Brunswick
EOA 2HO

Ferncliff Gardens
SS 1
Mission, British Columbia
V2V 5V6

McFayden Seed Co. Ltd.
Box 1800
Brandon, Manitoba
R7A 6N4

Stirling Perennials
RR 1
Morpeth, Ontario
N0P 1X0

AUSTRALIA

Country Farm Perennials
RSD Laings Road
Nayook VIC 3821

Cox's Nursery
RMB 216 Oaks Road
Thrilmere NSW 2572

Honeysuckle Cottage Nursery
Lot 35 Bowen Mountain Road
Bowen Mountain via Grosevale NSW 2753

Swan Bros Pty Ltd
490 Galston Road
Dural NSW 2158

FURTHER READING

GENERAL

The Complete Book of Plant Propagation, Graham Clarke and Alan Toogood. Ward Lock Ltd., 1992.

Controlling Weeds, Erin Hynes. Rodale Press, 1995.

Creative Propagation: A Grower's Guide, Peter Thompson. Timber Press, 1992.

The Dirt Doctor's Guide to Organic Gardening: Essays on the Natural Way, Howard Garrett. University of Texas Press, 1995.

The Garden Primer, Barbara Damrosch. Workman, 1988.

Great Garden Shortcuts: 100s of All-New Tips and Techniques That Guarantee You'll Save Time, Save Money, Save Work, Joan Benjamin and Erin Hynes. Rodale Press, 1996.

The Home Gardener's Source: The Ultimate Guide to Shopping for Your Garden by Mail, Fax, or Phone, Solomon M. Skolnick. Random House, 1997.

Let It Rot! The Gardener's Guide to Composting, Stu Campbell. Garden Way Publications, 1990.

The Organic Gardener's Handbook of Natural Insect and Disease Control. Rodale Press, 1992.

The Pruning Book, Lee Reich. Macmillan, 1997.

The Rodale Book of Composting, Deborah L. Martin and Grace Gershuny (Editor). Rodale Press, 1993.

Seed to Seed, Suzanne Ashworth. Seed Saver Publications, 1995.

Weathering Winter: A Gardener's Daybook, Carl H. Klaus. University of Iowa Press, 1997.

VEGETABLES

Heirloom Vegetable Gardening: A Master Gardener's Guide to Planting, Growing, Seed Saving, and Cultural History, William Woys Weaver. Henry Holt Co., 1997.

Heirloom Vegetables: A Home Gardener's Guide to Finding and Growing Vegetables from the Past, Sue Strickland, et al. Fireside, 1998.

The Salad Garden, Joy Larkcom and Roger Phillips. Penguin, 1996.

Taylor's Guide to Heirloom Vegetables, Benjamin Watson, ed. Houghton Mifflin, 1996.

Vegetable Gardening with Derek Fell, Derek Fell. Friedman/Fairfax Publishers, 1996.

HERBS

100 Favorite Herbs, Teri Dunn. Friedman/Fairfax Publishers, 1998.

The Complete Book of Herbs and Spices: An Illustrated Guide to Growing and Using Culinary, Aromatic, Cosmetic, and Medicinal Plants, Sarah Gardland. Reader's Digest, 1993.

Herbal Treasures: Inspiring Month-by-Month Projects for Gardening, Cooking, and Crafts, Phyllis V. Shaudys. Garden Way Publishing Co., 1990.

Herb Gardening with Derek Fell, Derek Fell. Friedman/Fairfax Publishers, 1997.

Herbs: An Illustrated Encyclopedia, Kathi Keville. Friedman/Fairfax Publishers, 1994.

A Modern Herbal, Volume 1, Maud Grieve. Dover Publications, 1978.

A Modern Herbal, Volume 2, Maud Grieve. Dover Publications, 1978.

The Potted Herb, Abbie Zabar. Stewart, Tabori, and Chang, 1988.

Taylor's Pocket Guide to Herbs and Edible Flowers, Norman Taylor and Ann Reilly. Houghton Mifflin, 1990.

FLOWERS

100 Favorite Perennials, Teri Dunn. Friedman/Fairfax Publishers, 1998.

American Horticultural Society Encyclopedia of Garden Plants, Christopher Brickell, ed. Macmillan, 1989.

From Seed to Bloom: How to Grow Over 500 Annuals, Perennials, and Herbs, Eileen Powell. Garden Way Publishing Co., 1995.

Perennial Gardening with Derek Fell, Derek Fell. Friedman/Fairfax Publishers, 1996.

FRUIT

The Backyard Berry Book: A Hands-On Guide to Growing Berries, Brambles, and Vine Fruit in the Home Garden, Stella Otto. Otto Graphics, 1995.

The Backyard Orchardist: A Complete Guide to Growing Fruit Trees in the Home Garden, Stella Otto. Otto Grapics, 1995.

The Fruit Expert, D.G. Hessayon. Sterling, 1991.

The Orchard Almanac: A Seasonal Guide to Healthy Fruit Trees, Steve Page, et al. Agaccess, 1996.

A Produce Reference Guide to Fruits and Vegetables from Around the World: Nature's Harvest. Donald D. Heaton. Food Products Press, 1997.

PRESERVING AND GARDEN CRAFTS

The Big Book of Preserving the Harvest, Carol Costenbader. Storey Publications, 1997.

The Book of Country Herbal Crafts: A Step-by-Step Guide to Making Over 100 Beautiful Wreaths, Garlands, Bouquets, and Much More, Dawn Cusick. Rodale Press, 1991.

Bountiful Blooms: Preserving Flowers with Colour, Margaret Burch. Sally Milner Publishing, 1994.

The Complete Guide to Home Preserving, Canning, and Freezing, The United States Department of Agriculture. Dover Publications, 1994.

Dried Flower Crafts: Capturing the Best of Your Garden to Decorate Your Home, Dawn Cusick. Rodale Press, 1996.

A Gift of Herbs: Easy-to-Make, Inexpensive and Thoughtful Gifts Using Herbs, Heidi Hartwiger. Down Home Press, 1993.

Gifts from the Herb Garden, Emelie Tolley and Chris Mead. Clarkson Potter, 1991.

Herb Drying Handbook: Includes Complete Microwave Drying Instructions, Nora Blose and Dawn Cusick. Sterling, 1993.

Harvesting, Preserving, and Arranging Dried Flowers, Cathy Miller and Rob Gray. Artisan, 1997.

Keeping the Harvest: Preserving Your Fruits, Vegetables, and Herbs, Nancy Chioffi, Gretchen Mead, and Linda M. Thompson. Storey Communications, 1991.

Scented Treasures: Aromatic Gifts from Your Kitchen and Garden, Stephanie Donaldson and Shona Wood. Storey Communications, 1996.

PLANT HARDINESS ZONES

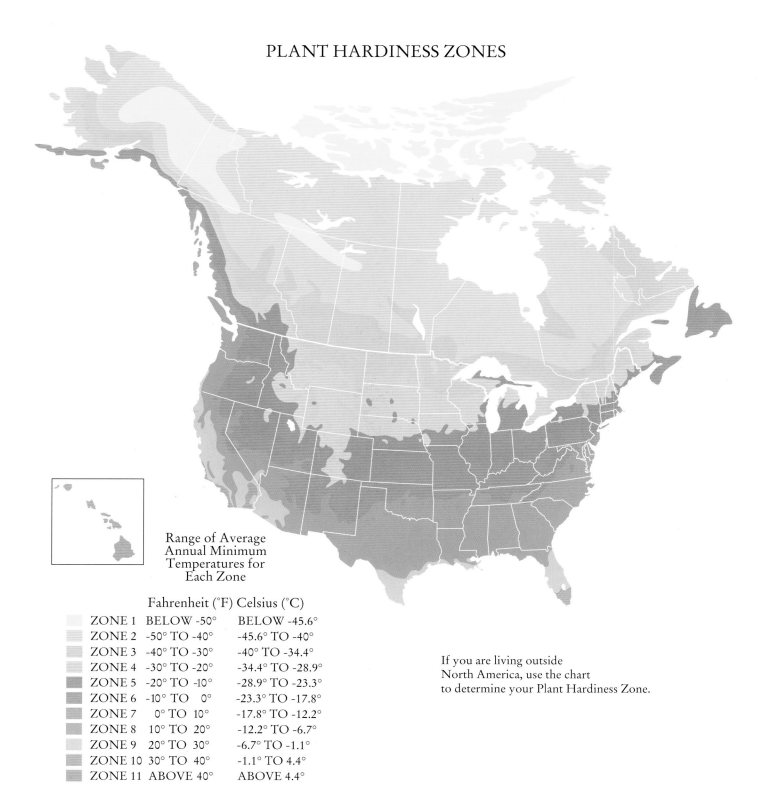

Range of Average
Annual Minimum
Temperatures for
Each Zone

	Fahrenheit (°F)	Celsius (°C)
ZONE 1	BELOW -50°	BELOW -45.6°
ZONE 2	-50° TO -40°	-45.6° TO -40°
ZONE 3	-40° TO -30°	-40° TO -34.4°
ZONE 4	-30° TO -20°	-34.4° TO -28.9°
ZONE 5	-20° TO -10°	-28.9° TO -23.3°
ZONE 6	-10° TO 0°	-23.3° TO -17.8°
ZONE 7	0° TO 10°	-17.8° TO -12.2°
ZONE 8	10° TO 20°	-12.2° TO -6.7°
ZONE 9	20° TO 30°	-6.7° TO -1.1°
ZONE 10	30° TO 40°	-1.1° TO 4.4°
ZONE 11	ABOVE 40°	ABOVE 4.4°

If you are living outside
North America, use the chart
to determine your Plant Hardiness Zone.

INDEX

PHOTOGRAPHY CREDITS

©R. Todd Davis: 1, 71 left, 78, 93, 96 right, 104 top, 112

©Derek Fell: 12, 14, 15, 19 top and bottom left, 20 both, 26 top and bottom left, 29 left, 62, 67 bottom, 80

©John Glover: 5, 7 top and bottom right, 10, 17, 24, 26 top right, 30 top left and bottom right, 48, 50 bottom, 54, 59, 65, 66, 67 top, 68-69, 72 left, 73, 74 top, 75, 81, 82, 84, 85, 86-87, 92 right, 94 both, 96 left, 108-109, 111, 114, 115, 116-117, 118, 119, 122 top right and bottom left and right, 123, 124, 125, 128, 129, 132

©Dency Kane: 7 top and bottom left, 28, 29 right, 32, 36, 51, 52, 55 top and bottom right, 57 left, 60, 61, 63 bottom, 74 bottom, 79, 88, 90, 104 bottom, 110, 126

©Lynn Karlin: 13, 19 right, 25, 49 top, 53, 56, 63 top, 70, 72 right, 83, 91, 95, 97, 98, 102, 106, 107 both, 120, 127, 130, 131

©Clive Nichols: endpapers (Old Rectory Northants), 2 (HMP Leyhill-Hampton Court), 6, 8 (Little Court, Crawley, Hants), 23 (HMP Leyhill-Hampton Court), 30 bottom left, 44 (Julie Toll), 49 bottom (HMP Leyhill-Hampton Court), 76-77 (Old Rectory Northants)

©Jerry Pavia: 35, 50 top, 54 bottom left, 58 left, 64, 71 right, 92 left, 99, 100-101, 105, 122 top left

©Joanne Pavia: 57 right, 58 right